ABRAHAM LINCOLN
The Man and the Myth

". . . that this nation, under God, shall have a new birth of freedom . . ." (Gettysburg Address, 1863)

CREATORS OF THE AMERICAN MIND
VOLUME 3

ABRAHAM LINCOLN

The Man and the Myth

James T. Baker

Western Kentucky University

Harcourt College Publishers

Fort Worth   Philadelphia   San Diego   New York   Orlando   Austin
San Antonio   Toronto   Montreal   London   Sydney   Tokyo

Publisher	Earl McPeek
Acquisitions Editor	David Tatom
Market Strategist	Steve Drummond
Developmental Editor	Margaret McAndrew Beasley
Project Editor	G. Parrish Glover
Art Director	Chris Morrow
Production Manager	Diane Gray

ISBN: 0-15-505699-9

Library of Congress Catalog Card Number: 99-65282

Address for Domestic Orders
Harcourt College Publishers, 6277 Sea Harbor Drive, Orlando, FL 32887-6777
800-782-4479

Address for International Orders
International Customer Service
Harcourt, Inc., 6277 Sea Harbor Drive, Orlando, FL 32887-6777
407-345-3800
(fax) 407-345-4060
(e-mail) hbintl@harcourtbrace.com

Address for Editorial Correspondence
Harcourt College Publishers, 301 Commerce Street, Suite 3700, Fort Worth, TX 76102

Web Site Address
http://www.harcourtcollege.com

Printed in the United States of America

9 0 1 2 3 4 5 6 7 8 066 9 8 7 6 5 4 3 2 1

For MacBrennan Bailey and Chandler Hiett
All good fortune in the new century.

PREFACE

Abraham Lincoln: The Man and the Myth, is one in a series of books collectively called *Creators of the American Mind*.

ABOUT THE SERIES

Many historians believe that despite great diversity among the American people, despite our racial, religious, and cultural differences, there is such a thing as an American Mind: molded by a common history, common hopes and dreams, common fears and concerns. Even when Americans quarrel, the American Mind provides them with subjects and ammunition for their arguments.

It is the thesis of this series of books that certain individuals (political, religious, intellectual leaders, male and female, of all ethnic groups) have through their ideas and deeds helped create this American mind. Americans, whether they admire, despise, or even know what these creators said and did, reflect in their own thoughts and actions the imprint these persons left on our history. This series spotlights some of the Creators of the American Mind, listening when possible to their own words, comparing the sometimes conflicting opinions of their biographers, juxtaposing their supporters and critics, all in an attempt to see how, why, and to what degree each one contributed to the development of an American way of thought and deed. The subject of this volume, Abraham Lincoln, is certainly a central figure in this development, a principle actor in the drama of American history, a Creator of the American Mind.

ABOUT THIS VOLUME

This book, I believe, offers an accurate but novel approach to Lincoln and his place in American history.

1. It presents Lincoln as a man, a flesh-and-blood individual, by letting him speak for himself and by providing comments about him by his contemporaries as well as by Lincoln scholars who have studied him from various historical perspectives. Students learn both the facts of Lincoln's life and the way prominent historians interpret those facts.

2. It places Lincoln in historical perspective by following his rise through nineteenth-century history and politics, his conduct of the Civil War while he was President, the act of emancipation of the slaves, his assassination and its effects on the nation, his posthumous elevation to a central place in American political mythology, all using contemporary documents and the writings of Lincoln scholars.

3. It demonstrates, using the words of poets and orators as well as the assessments of historians, how Lincoln, after his tragic death, came to reflect the highest ideals of the Americans who followed him, how seen from the perspective of his "martyrdom" to the cause of national unity, he became a Creator of the American Mind.

4. It analyzes, as objectively as can be done, the intriguing myth of Lincoln the "Redeemer" of the "American Political Religion," showing the place Lincoln holds in the pageant of American history.

5. It offers, at appropriate intervals, analyses of the material being examined, summations of that material, and questions that teachers and students may use for responsive, reflective essays or discussions of the material.

6. It offers at the end of the book a number of topics for extended essays and/or term papers on all of the materials in the volume. Under this one cover should be enough information of sufficiently varying topics for students to do different research projects on Lincoln the Man, Lincoln the Liberator, and Lincoln the Redeemer.

7. It provides a selected annotated bibliography on Lincoln so that students may dig more deeply into areas of Lincoln's life covered briefly or merely suggested in the book itself.

This book is long enough to present a complete picture of Lincoln the Man and Myth yet brief enough to serve as a supplement to a larger textbook on American history, for courses in American History Survey, American Social and Intellectual History, and the History of Religion in America.

ACKNOWLEDGMENTS

The author is grateful to the following reviewers who read this book in manuscript form and made many corrective and constructive suggestions on how to make it more accurate, inclusive, and useful to teachers and students: Stacy A. Cordery, Monmouth College; Raymond Hyser, James Madison University; James R. Kluger, Pima Community College; Michael L. Krenn, University of Miami; Alice E. Reagan, Northern Virginia Community College; R. B. Rosenburg, University of North Alabama.

Thanks also to the Faculty Research committee of Western Kentucky University, Elmer Gray, Chairman, for funds to help bring this project to completion; to Liz Jensen who made it technically presentable; to Drake Bush, David Tatom, Margaret Beasley, Parrish Glover, Diane Gray, and Chris Morrow of Harcourt College Publishers who gave it encouragement and direction; and to my daughters Virginia and Elizabeth and to Virginia's son MacBrennan and Elizabeth's son Chandler.

CONTENTS

CHRONOLOGY

1809   Born February 12, near Hodgenville, Kentucky

1816   Moves with family to Indiana; mother dies and father marries Sarah Johnston

1818–22 Attends school sporadically

1830   Moves to Illinois, first Decatur, then New Salem; makes first political speeches

1832   Participates in the Black Hawk War; loses race for the Illinois General Assembly

1834   Elected to the Illinois legislature as a Whig; begins study of law, which leads to passing the bar examination

1842   Marries Mary Todd of Kentucky; does not seek reelection to the legislature

1847–49 Serves in thirtieth United States Congress as a Whig; publicly opposes war with Mexico; voluntarily steps down after the one term

1850   Death of son Edward; beginning of mid-life changes

1856   Helps found the Illinois Republican Party

1858   Nominated by the Republican Party for the United States Senate; debates Stephen A. Douglas; loses race but gains national reputation as opponent of extending slavery to the territories

1860   Elected president of the United States

1861   Inaugurated as president; outbreak of the Civil War

1863   Issues Emancipation Proclamation on January 1

1864   Elected to a second presidential term

1865   War ends on April 9; Lincoln shot on April 14 while attending a play at Ford's Theater; dies on April 15; Thirteenth Amendment to Constitution, ending slavery, is adopted after his death

INTRODUCTION

Abraham Lincoln, the sixteenth president of the United States, stands at the center of American history and civilization. The great Civil War of 1861–65 which threatened to divide the nation permanently, a war that occupied all of Lincoln's years as president, might have come to pass had he not been elected in 1860, but without Lincoln's personality and leadership the outcome would doubtless have been quite different, and without him the way in which Americans have come to remember and assess the meaning of that war would certainly be less positive.

The American Mind, a term I have chosen to represent the way Americans as a people collectively think about their nation—its past, its present, its future, and its place in world history—cannot be fully understood and explained without carefully examining how Lincoln's words and deeds affected American history. A politician from what was then the western state of Illinois, a man who opposed the extension of slavery into unsettled territories but who doubted that it could be abolished constitutionally, struck the most powerful blow possible against it when he issued the Emancipation Proclamation on January 1, 1863. The Thirteenth Amendment to the Constitution, which he helped start on its way to passage before his untimely death, forever ended slavery, removing what most Americans now believe to be the deepest stain on our political system. The name most closely associated with this conviction of the American Mind is Abraham Lincoln.

Because Lincoln died from an assassin's bullet at the very moment that victory in the war to preserve the Union had been assured, killed by a man opposed both to the Union and to freedom for the slaves, he was transformed almost immediately into a figure of mythic proportions. During his years in the political spotlight, even during his time in the White House, he was a man more abused than praised. His election was an immediate cause of the secession of the Southern states. He had trouble controlling his own political coalition, with strong minds on one side demanding swifter action to abolish slavery and those on the other cautioning against swift action. He had trouble winning a war in which his side had the strongest odds but his own generals often disappointed him militarily or showed him little respect. He had trouble keeping the border states of Maryland, Kentucky, and Missouri loyal to the Union, despite taking strong measures against them, at times suspending civil liberties in violation of the Constitution. He even had some trouble winning a second term as president because the war went on so long and was so costly. But his ultimate victory, followed so closely by what Americans immediately began to think of as his martyrdom to the causes of emancipation and unity, changed everything. Even before his burial in April, 1865, Lincoln was on his way to legendary greatness.

As we shall see in this book, many historians who follow American intellectual and religious development believe that, perhaps unconsciously, we share a common "political religion." While many citizens take part in a variety of religions, which differ widely in their tenets and forms of worship, and while we may disagree strongly about matters of faith or doctrine, we all give allegiance to a common form of civil religion. In this religion, which keeps us united as a nation, the nation is our church, the flag our cross, and the president our high priest. Believers and nonbelievers alike accept the ideals of this political religion because of the power it has to bind a diverse nation together. In the scheme of our political religion, Abraham Lincoln has become more than president-priest: he has become the Redeemer.

Lincoln's elevation to the role of martyr to the causes of liberation and national unity, then to political sainthood, and finally to redeemer of the American nation began as his body lay in state and made its long, slow journey cross country to burial in Illinois. We know that Lincoln did not intend to die for his country and its ideals. He talked just days before he was killed of his plans, once free of the presidency in 1869, to make a tour of the world and then to settle down to practice law and earn enough money to live comfortably in his old age. Death ended his plans, but it also silenced his detractors. Freed slaves, Northerners who had criticized Lincoln for acting too slowly or too quickly regarding slavery, and even many Southerners, who only reluctantly complied with his plan to restore their status as fellow Americans—a wide majority came to revere him. They acknowledged that this man with little formal education had left a political, literary, and moral legacy that outshone those of all previous presidents and deserved to be featured on Mount Rushmore with George Washington, Thomas Jefferson, and Theodore Roosevelt.

In the four sections that follow we will trace Lincoln's rise to power, his achievements as the nation's leader, his pivotal decision to emancipate the slaves, and his elevation to the highest summit of "religious" influence after his death. We will also be able to understand how and why he became one of the most important of the creators of the American Mind.

—

PART I

Lincoln the Man

Behind the myth of Abraham Lincoln, behind the image of the greatest president, behind Lincoln the Great Emancipator, behind his role as redeemer in the American political religion, lies Lincoln the man and citizen. The real flesh-and-blood Abraham Lincoln—who was he? The answer to this question is complicated by the fact that Lincoln kept no journal and left no autobiography beyond scattered comments and jottings. Although historians try to capture him in their verbal portraits, they face a bewildering body of conflicting testimony and present contradictory assessments of who and what he was.

In his own time Lincoln was called a clumsy buffoon and a graceful, consummate actor. He was said to be a shameless opportunist and a man of firm convictions. He was condemned as cautious to the point of cowardice and praised as courageous to the point of heroism. In the end, each person must discover and judge Lincoln individually. Yet there is plenty of help. Many writers have published portraits of Lincoln, and we will make use of them to help form our conclusions.

THE IMAGE

The invention of photography in the 1830s—and its vast improvement by the 1860s—made Lincoln the first nationally recognizable president and one of the most familiar figures in U.S.

history. Several accomplished photographers, particularly Matthew Brady, captured his image for posterity.

There are also many written portraits of Lincoln. He has been the subject of more articles and books than any other American, president or not. Some of his biographers have been unabashed admirers, some have judged him critically, but all have added to his collective image. One of the earliest writers to attempt a biography was Lincoln's law partner during his days in Illinois just before his election to the presidency, William H. Herndon. Lincoln's third law partner in Springfield, and a conscientious and careful man, Herndon wrote his biography of Lincoln during the quarter century after his assassination, when Lincoln was rising to mythical stature. Knowing more about Lincoln's life before 1860 than any other biographer, Herndon tried to present an honest, accurate account of the man and his life, but he was nonetheless influenced by the events of Lincoln's presidency, his tragic assassination, and his rise in popular opinion to virtual sainthood. In the following excerpt from his book *Abraham Lincoln: The True Story of a Great Life*, first published in 1892, Herndon describes Lincoln's physical appearance and personality.

> Mr. Lincoln was six feet four inches high, and when he left the city of his home for Washington was fifty-one years old, having good health and no gray hairs, or but few, on his head. He was thin, wiry, sinewy, raw-boned; thin through the breast to the back, and narrow across the shoulders; standing he leaned forward—was what may be called stoop-shouldered, inclining to the consumptive by build. His usual weight was one hundred and eighty pounds. His organization—rather his structure and functions—worked slowly. His blood had to run a long distance from his heart to the extremities of his frame, and his nerve force had to travel through dry ground a long distance before his muscles were obedient to his will. His structure was loose and leathery; his body was shrunk and shriveled; he had dark skin, dark hair, and looked woe-struck. The whole man, body and mind, worked slowly, as if it needed oiling. Physically he was a very powerful man, lifting with ease four hundred, and in one case six hundred, pounds. His mind was like his body, and worked slowly but strongly. Hence there was very little bodily or mental wear and tear in him. This peculiarity in his construction gave him great advantage over other men in public life. No man in America—scarcely a man in the world—could have stood what Lincoln did in Washington and survived through more than one term of the Presidency.
>
> When he walked he moved cautiously but firmly; his long arms and giant hands swung down by his side. He walked with even tread,

the inner sides of his feet being parallel. He put the whole foot flat down on the ground at once, not landing on the heel; he likewise lifted his foot all at once, not rising from the toe, and hence he had no spring to his walk. His walk was undulatory—catching and pocketing tire, weariness, and pain, all up and down his person, and thus preventing them from locating. The first impression of a stranger, or a man who did not observe closely, was that his walk implied shrewdness and cunning—that he was a tricky man; but, in reality, it was the walk of caution and firmness. In sitting down on a common chair he was no taller than ordinary men. His legs and arms were abnormally, unnaturally long, and in undue proportion to the remainder of his body. It was only when he stood up that he loomed above other men.

Mr. Lincoln's head was long, and tall from the base of the brain and from the eyebrows. His head ran backwards, his forehead rising as it ran back at a low angle, like Clay's, and unlike Webster's, which was almost perpendicular. The size of his hat measured at the hatter's block was seven and one-eighth, his head being, from ear to ear, six and one-half inches, and from the front to the back of the brain eight inches. Thus measured it was not below the medium size. His forehead was narrow but high; his hair was dark, almost black, and lay floating where his fingers or the winds left it, piled up at random. His cheek-bones were high, sharp, and prominent; his jaws were long and upcurved; his nose was large, long, blunt, and a little awry towards the right eye; his chin was sharp and upcurved; his eyebrows cropped out like a huge rock on the brow of a hill; his long, sallow face was wrinkled and dry, with a hair here and there on the surface; his cheeks were leathery; his ears were large, and ran out almost at right angles from his head, caused partly by heavy hats and partly by nature; his lower lip was thick, hanging, and undercurved, while his chin reached for the lip upcurved; his neck was neat and trim, his head being well balanced on it; there was the lone mole on the right cheek, and Adam's apple on his throat.

Thus stood, walked, acted, and looked Abraham Lincoln. He was not a pretty man by any means, nor was he an ugly one; he was a homely man, careless of his looks, plain-looking and plain-acting. He had no pomp, display, or dignity, so-called. He appeared simple in his carriage and bearing. He was a sad-looking man; his melancholy dripped from him as he walked. His apparent gloom impressed his friends, and created sympathy for him—one means of his great success. He was gloomy, abstracted, and joyous—rather humorous—by turns; but I do not think he knew what real joy was for many years.

In a footnote Herndon speculated about Lincoln's sadness.

Lincoln's melancholy never failed to impress any man who ever saw or knew him. The perpetual look of sadness was his most prominent feature. The cause of this peculiar condition was a matter of frequent discussion among his friends. John T. Stuart said it was due to his abnormal digestion. His liver failed to work properly—did not se-crete bile—and his bowels were equally as inactive. "I used to advise him to take blue-mass pills," related Stuart, "and he did take them before he went to Washington, and for five months while he was President, but when it came on to Congress he told me he had ceased using them because they made him cross." The reader can hardly realize the extent of this peculiar tendency to gloom. One of Lincoln's colleagues in the Legislature of Illinois is authority for the statement coming from Lincoln himself that this "mental depression became so intense at times he never dared carry a pocket knife." Two things greatly intensified his characteristic sadness; one was the endless succession of troubles in his domestic life, which he had to bear in silence; and the other was unquestionably the knowledge of his own obscure and lowly origin. The recollection of these things burned a deep impress on his sensitive soul.

As to the cause of this morbid condition my idea has always been that it was occult, and could not be explained by any course of observation and reasoning. It was ingrained, and, being ingrained, could not be reduced to rule, or the cause arrayed. It was necessarily hereditary, but whether it came down from a long line of ancestors and far back, or was simply the reproduction of the saddened life of Nancy Hanks, cannot well be determined. At any rate it was part of his nature, and could no more be shaken off than he could part with his brains.

YOUNG MAN LINCOLN

Lincoln's early life is familiar to most schoolchildren because it provides so many examples of how a successful person must tri-umph over adversity. Lincoln was born in 1809 in a log cabin in Kentucky to a farm family that had come from Virginia. He grew up in what today would be described as grinding poverty. The family moved to Indiana when Lincoln was seven. There his mother Nancy died, and young Abe gained a stepmother before he was ten. His father, Thomas, then moved the family to Illinois, where Lincoln grew to manhood.

While Lincoln is often pictured doing physical labor—"the rail splitter" is a familiar image of him—as a young man he actually hated farming and its related chores, and he made every effort to escape the life his father pursued. He received at most a total of two years of formal education; but he taught himself to read and write fluently, although his spelling always left much to be de-sired. His stepmother, Sally, recalled that he especially loved to read the newspapers, which were just making an appearance on the frontier.

Lincoln also showed an early interest in politics and began at twenty-one to throw his hat into the ring for various offices. He proved to be an effective stump speaker and door-to-door campaigner with his impressive height, a ready smile, and usually a humorous story to illustrate the point he wanted to make. At the age of twenty-five he was elected to the Illinois state legislature.

He also read books on the law, aiming at a career in which he could use his mind rather than his body to earn a living, and he qualified through self-education for the bar. He became a successful prairie lawyer, at first traveling long distances on a circuit to try cases, then settling in Springfield to conduct a law practice with William H. Herndon.

It appears that Lincoln from his youth cultivated a keen sense of humor and was known for his vivid, colorful storytelling, both of which helped his legal and political pursuits. Herndon once remarked that Lincoln used stories because he lacked a strong vocabulary, and that he read less but thought more than any great man of history. While acknowledging his frequent use of stories, particularly humorous ones, to make his point, Lincoln said he did not invent but merely borrowed them. Senator Charles Sumner of Massachusetts said Lincoln told him that he had "no invention, only a good memory" for anecdotes. Anthony Gross quotes Lincoln on the subject in his book *Lincoln's Own Stories:* "You speak of Lincoln stories. I don't think that is a correct phrase. I don't make the stories mine by telling them. I'm only a retail dealer."

Whether he was an inventor or merely a retailer, Lincoln's stories became his trademark, and they helped him win cases and offices. They were generally earthy and humorous. Some of his relatives believed he learned his art of humorous storytelling from his father, Thomas, who was also famous for anecdotal arguments, but Lincoln, who did not like his father and the farm work he made Lincoln do, did not credit him.

One of Abraham Lincoln's best stories from his early life, recounted by Anthony Gross, came from his one military experience, when he was a citizen-officer in the 1832 Indian uprising in Illinois called the Black Hawk War. He was drilling his men twenty abreast across a field when they approached a fence with a narrow gate. "I could not for the life of me remember the proper word of command for getting my company 'endwise,' so that it could get through the gate," he later recalled when illustrating his lack of military experience and his ineptitude at command. "So, as we came near the gate, I shouted: This company is dismissed for two minutes, when it will fall in again on the other side of the gate."

LINCOLN AS HUSBAND AND FATHER

From age twenty-five to thirty-three Lincoln served in the Illinois legislature and practiced law, living as a bachelor. He was, however, no monk. He courted several women, among them Ann Rutledge, whom many believed he would have married had she not died in 1835.

In 1842 he met, courted, and won the hand in marriage of Mary Todd, a woman from an aristocratic Kentucky family. Mary was diminutive in contrast to Abraham's six-feet four-inch frame, but her personality loomed large in their relationship. She often made his life difficult, as the following comments of Lincoln's partner Herndon make clear, but she certainly helped mold the Lincoln she married into the Lincoln of history.

> When Mr. Lincoln entered the domain of investigation he was a severe and persistent thinker, and had wonderful endurance; hence he was abstracted, and for that reason at times was somewhat unsocial, reticent, and uncommunicative. After his marriage it cannot be said that he liked the society of ladies; in fact, it was just what he did not like, though one of his biographers says otherwise. Lincoln had none of the tender ways that please a woman, and he could not, it seemed, by any positive act of his own make her happy. If his wife was happy, she was naturally happy, or made herself so in spite of countless drawbacks. He was, however, a good husband in his own peculiar way, and in his own way only.
>
> If exhausted from severe and long-continued thought, he had to touch the earth again to renew his strength. When this weariness set in he would stop thought, and get down and play with a little dog or kitten to recover; and when the recovery came he would push it aside to play with its own tail. He treated men and women in much the same way. For fashionable society he had a marked dislike, although he appreciated its value in promoting the welfare of a man ambitious to succeed in politics. If he was invited out to dine or to mingle in some social gathering, and came in contact with the ladies, he treated them with becoming politeness; but the

consciousness of his shortcomings as a society man rendered him unusually diffident, and at the very first opportunity he would have the men separated from their ladies and crowded close around him in one corner of the parlor, listening to one of his characteristic stories. That a lady as proud and as ambitious to exercise the rights of supremacy in society as Mary Todd should repent of her marriage to the man I have just described surely need occasion no surprise in the mind of any one. Both she and the man whose hand she accepted acted along the lines of human conduct, and both reaped the bitter harvest of conjugal infelicity. In dealing with Mr. Lincoln's home life perhaps I am revealing an element of his character that has heretofore been kept from the world; but in doing so I feel sure I am treading on no persons' toes, for all the actors in this domestic drama are dead, and the world seems ready to hear the facts. As his married life, in the opinion of all his friends, exerted a peculiar influence over Mr. Lincoln's political career there can be no impropriety, I apprehend, in throwing the light on it now . . . one of her greatest misfortunes was her inability to control her temper. Admit that, and everything can be explained. However cold and abstracted her husband may have appeared to others, however impressive, when aroused, may have seemed his indignation in public, he never gave vent to his feelings at home. He always meekly accepted as final the authority of his wife in all matters of domestic concern.[1] This may explain somewhat the statement of Judge Davis[2] that "as a general rule, when all the lawyers of a Saturday evening would go home and see their families and friends, Lincoln would find some excuse and refuse to go. We said nothing but it seemed to us all he was not domestically happy." He exercised no government of any kind over his household. His children did much as they pleased. Many of their antics he approved, and he restrained them in nothing. He never reproved them or gave them a fatherly frown. He was the most indulgent parent I have ever known. He was in the habit, when at home on Sunday, of bringing his two boys, Willie and Thomas—or "Tad"—down to the office to remain while his wife attended church. He seldom accompanied her there. The boys were absolutely unrestrained in their amusement. If they pulled down all the books from the shelves, bent the points of all the pens, overtured inkstands, scattered law papers over the floor,

---

[1] Herndon added this footnote: One day a man making some improvements in Lincoln's yard suggested to Mrs. Lincoln the propriety of cutting down one of the trees, to which she willingly assented. Before doing so, however, the man came down to our office and consulted Lincoln himself about it. "What did Mrs. Lincoln say?" enquired the latter. "She consented to have it taken away." "Then, in God's name," exclaimed Lincoln, "cut it down to the roots!"

[2] David Davis was a personal friend of both Abraham and Mary Todd Lincoln. Davis was appointed a justice of the Supreme Court by President Lincoln.

Abraham and Mary Todd Lincoln, the rising lawyer and his wife, the

or threw the pencils into the spittoon, it never disturbed the serenity of their father's good-nature. Frequently absorbed in thought, he never observed their mischievous but destructive pranks—as his unfortunate partner did, who thought much, but said nothing—and, even if brought to his attention, he virtually encouraged their repetition by declining to show any substantial evidence of parental disapproval. After church was over the boys and their father, climbing down the office stairs, ruefully turned their steps homeward. They mingled with the throngs of well-dressed people returning from church, the majority of whom might well have wondered if the trio they passed were going to a fireside where love and white-winged peace reigned supreme. A near relative of Mrs. Lincoln, in explanation of the unhappy condition of things in that lady's household, offered this suggestion: "Mrs. Lincoln came of the best stock, and was raised

way they looked while raising their family in Springfield, Illinois.

like a lady. Her husband was her opposite in origin, in education, in breeding, in everything; and it is therefore quite natural that she should complain if he answered the door-bell himself instead of sending the servant to do so; neither is able to be condemned if, as you say, she raised 'merry war' because he persisted in using his own knife in the butter, instead of the silver-handled one intended for that purpose." Such want of social polish on the part of her husband of course gave Mrs. Lincoln great offense, and therefore in commenting on it she cared neither for time nor place. Her frequent outbursts of temper precipitated many an embarrassment for which Lincoln with great difficulty extricated himself.

It is evident from his selection of memories and his tone that Herndon did not like Mrs. Lincoln. Nevertheless, much of what he writes is corroborated by other contemporary observers.

The Lincoln marriage produced four children, all sons. Robert Todd was born in 1843, a year after their marriage, and lived until 1926, the only one of the Lincoln sons to reach adulthood. He was in college during much of his father's time in the White House, and he was estranged from his mother in her later years as he tried to have her institutionalized for mental instability. Edward Baker lived only from 1846 to 1850. William Wallace, born in 1850 after Edward's death, died in 1862 at the White House, probably from the contaminated water of the Potomac, on whose shores various army battalions camped. Thomas, called Tad, born in 1853 with an enlarged head and cleft palate, died in 1871 at age eighteen.

Herndon said that Lincoln was an indulgent father who "exercised no government at all" over his sons, just as he did not over his wife. The boys did pretty much as they pleased, without paternal restraint, Lincoln seeming to approve of their antics, considering them evidence of masculine good health. He once wrote: "It is my pleasure that my children are free and happy, and unrestrained by parental tyranny. Love is the chain, whereby to bind a child to its parents."

Mary Todd Lincoln, the Kentucky woman who married beneath herself, became first lady of the United States in 1861, when her commoner husband became president. In the White House she far outspent her allotted budget trying to prove that she was not the unsophisticated frontier woman she feared eastern women would call her. She continued both to bless and curse Lincoln's life in Washington. As first lady during the Civil War, married to perhaps America's most important president, she is because of fate one of our most famous first ladies and because of personality one of the most discussed and controversial.

LINCOLN THE LAWYER

Lincoln was a successful lawyer, especially given that he was almost completely self-educated. Herndon, who had plenty of opportunity to observe Lincoln in his practice of law, wrote a carefully measured analysis of the future president's strengths and weaknesses as a lawyer. Note that while Herndon considered Lincoln lacking in training, knowledge, and technique, he greatly admired his mind—its clarity, its tenacity, and its focus.

I easily realized that Lincoln was strikingly deficient in the technical rules of the law. Although he was constantly reminding young legal aspirants to study and "work, work," yet I doubt if he ever read a single elementary law book through in his life. In fact, I may truthfully say, I never knew him to read through a law book of any kind. Practically, he knew nothing of the rules of evidence, of pleading, or practice, as laid down in the text-books, and seemed to care nothing about them. He had a keen sense of justice, and struggled for it, throwing aside forms, methods, and rules, until it appeared pure as a ray of light flashing through a fog-bank. He was not a general reader in any field of knowledge, but when he had occasion to learn or investigate any subject he was thorough and indefatigable in his search. He not only went to the root of a question, but dug up the root, and separated and analyzed every fibre of it. He was in every respect a case lawyer, never cramming himself on any question till he had a case in which the question was involved. He thought slowly and acted slowly; he must needs have time to analyze all the facts in a case and wind them into a connected story. I have seen him lose cases of the plainest justice, which the most inexperienced member of the bar would have gained without effort. Two things were essential to his success in managing a case. One was time, the other a feeling of confidence in the justice of the cause he represented. He used to say, "If I can free this case from technicalities and get it properly swung to the jury, I'll win it." But if either of these essentials were lacking, he was the weakest man at the bar. He was greatest in my opinion as a lawyer in the Supreme Court of Illinois. There the cases were never hurried. The attorneys generally prepared their cases in the form of briefs, and the movements of the court and counsel were so slow that no one need be caught by surprise. I was with Lincoln once and listened to an oral argument by him in which he rehearsed an extended history of the law. It was a carefully prepared and masterly discourse, but, as I thought, entirely useless. After he was through and we were walking home I asked him why he went so far back in the history of the law. I presumed the court knew enough history. "That's where you're mistaken," was his instant rejoinder. "I dared not trust the case on the presumption that the court knows everything—in fact I argued it on the presumption that the court didn't know anything," a statement which, when one reviews the decision of our appellate courts, is not so extravagant as one would at first suppose.

I used to grow restless at Lincoln's slow movements and speeches in court. "Speak with more vim," I would frequently say, "and arouse the jury—talk faster and keep them awake." In answer to such a suggestion he one day made use of this illustration: "Give me your little pen-knife, with its short blade, and hand me that old jack-knife lying on the table." Opening the blade of the pen-knife he said: "You see, this blade at the point travels rapidly, but only through a small portion of space till it stops; while the long blade of

> the jack knife moves no faster but through a much greater space than the small one. Just so with the long, labored movements of my mind. I may not emit ideas as rapidly as others, because I am compelled by nature to speak slowly, but when I do throw off a thought it seems to me, though it comes with some effort, it has force enough to cut its own way and travel a greater distance." This was said to me when we were alone in our office simply for illustration. It was not said boastingly.

Anthony Gross included among his anecdotes and sayings about and by Lincoln one that seems to substantiate Herndon's assessment. Someone once remarked to Lincoln that he had a wonderfully quick mind, one on which impressions were easily made and never effaced. Lincoln replied that the first part was wrong. "I am slow to learn and slow to forget that which I have learned. My mind is like a piece of steel—very hard to scratch anything on it, and almost impossible, after you get it there, to rub it out." Such a mind made Lincoln the lawyer he was. It was the same mind that made him the president he was.

LINCOLN IN CONGRESS AND HIS "MID-LIFE CRISIS": THE BURLINGAME THESIS

Having served in the Illinois legislature until his marriage, then having helped to build up the Whig Party as he earned a living at law, Lincoln in 1846 ran successfully for Congress. He took his seat in the United States House of Representatives as a Whig the next year.

For a newcomer, Lincoln was an active and vocal congressman. He tended to the local interests of his Illinois district by introducing and supporting road projects that would bring prosperity to his region. He strongly opposed Democratic President James K. Polk's request for a declaration of war against Mexico in 1847, believing American action in south Texas aggressive and provocative. He doubted Polk's contention that Mexico had attacked U.S. troops; he demanded in a speech that Polk identify "the spot" where American blood had first been shed without provocation, and he accused Democrats of wanting a war in order to take warm-weather Mexican lands where slavery could be extended westward.

Although this opposition to U.S. foreign policy was not universally popular, Lincoln could probably have been reelected in 1848. The Whig candidate for president, Zachary Taylor, won the White House that year, and the Whig candidate carried his district in Illinois, but Lincoln declined to run. Had he pursued his congressional career, he might have become a successful national legislator, but perhaps not president, since Congress in those days was not a favorable training ground for the executive office.

Instead, Lincoln cited the Whig notion that offices should be rotated and refused to be a candidate for reelection. In 1849 he went home to his family and was apparently ready, at age forty, to leave political life behind him, saying he was "disgusted" with politics, and convinced that in the field of government he was at best a mediocrity. In 1850 his second son, Edward, died, a third son William was born, and Lincoln settled into a routine of hard work, self-examination, and recurring bouts of severe depression, which his close friends referred to in hushed tones as his "sadness."

The years 1849 to 1854, from Lincoln's "retirement" from public life to his reemergence as a reinvigorated public figure, saw a profound change in Lincoln's personality, interests, and convictions. During those years he rarely stood for any political office—and failed the few times he did—yet he entered those five years as essentially a small-town politician and emerged a statesman. Some say that he faced and eventually won out over a "mid-life crisis."

One of the best analyses of this crisis has been done by historian Michael Burlingame in his book *The Inner World of Abraham Lincoln*. Burlingame used principles of psychology to analyze the changes we see in the Lincoln who reappeared from obscurity in 1854. Such psychohistory is often regarded with suspicion because some practitioners have gone too far in attributing historical events to the psychological motives of the persons involved in them, often using questionable Freudian theories of human personality to prove their theses. Burlingame avoids such excesses, basing his theory about Lincoln's mid-life crisis on recorded facts and statements.

In the excerpt from his book that follows, Burlingame builds upon the theory that Lincoln, like many men around the age of forty, underwent a crisis of identity, as his youth faded and old age loomed, and that he successfully met this crisis through *individuation*, a term coined by psychologist Carl Jung to describe the way a person at mid-life learns to accept his or her own unique personality and potential. Burlingame describes individuation this way:

> Individuation at mid-life requires several things of a man: to reappraise his past; to ask fundamental questions about what is truly important; to develop atrophied areas of his psyche; to abandon inappropriate qualities of youthfulness and accept appropriate aspects of aging; to acknowledge and integrate the dark, destructive qualities of his self as well as the feminine components of his total personality; to pay more attention to his inner voice and less attention to the outer voice of the collective; to let go of some of his attachment to the external world; to become a mentor to younger men; to come to terms with his mortality; and to find his true calling and fully engage his creative gifts. This is a tall order indeed, and most men experience either a moderate or severe crisis as they try to fill it. If successful, a man emerges from this crisis less egocentric and more conscious, rooted, centered in himself, creative, and self-accepting.

Burlingame goes on to analyze and draw the following conclusions about this significant five-year period in Lincoln's middle years.

> A significant challenge in midlife is developing the weakest part of the psyche. According to Jung, everyone has four psychological functions: thinking, feeling, intuition, and sensation. One is dominant, one is inferior, and the other two are auxiliary. Clearly, Lincoln's strongest function was thinking, as his fondness for Euclid suggests. At the age of twenty-eight he enunciated a thinker's credo: "Reason, cold, calculating, unimpassioned reason, must furnish all the materials for our future support and defence." His fellow lawyers marveled at his powerful, analytical mind. One recalled that "the quality in which he excelled all other men was that of analysis. In the crucible of his mind every question was resolved into its pristine elements." Herndon thought that "Lincoln was entirely logical, had no intuition at all."
>
> According to Jung, "When thinking is the dominant or superior function, feeling is necessarily an inferior function." In Jung's typology, feeling is a rational enterprise that assigns value: "Feeling informs you through its feeling-tone whether a thing is agreeable or not. It tells you what a thing is *worth* to you." James Hillman[3] has noted that "the feeling function on a more primitive level is mainly a reaction of yes and no, like and dislike, acceptance and rejection. As it develops, there forms in us a subtle appreciation of values, and even of value systems, and our judgments of feeling then rest more and more on a rational hierarchy, whether it be in the realm of

---

[3] Hillman is a psychologist and author of *Healing Fiction.*

aesthetic taste, ethical goods, or social forms and human relation-ships. . . . The developed feeling function is the reason of the heart which the reason of the mind does not quite understand."

Between 1849 and 1854, Lincoln apparently struggled to de-velop his feeling function, especially in the realm of political values. Before 1849 he was something of a hack politician, stressing parti-sanship above all else. To be sure, he had expressed aversion to slav-ery, but he had not worked out a thorough or deep analysis of the peculiar institution. By 1854 he had done so, and his Peoria [Illinois] speech that year examined the issue with more than "cold, calculat-ing, unimpassioned reason." Heatedly he denounced as well as ana-lyzed the proslavery and popular sovereignty arguments, and for the rest of his life continued with passion to attack slavery as "a vast moral evil" and "the sum of all villa[i]nies." That he did so immedi-ately after his return to politics suggests that he used the five years of his semiretirement not only to study the issue, but also to assimilate his feeling function as he addressed it.

Another major task of the midlife transition is to acknowledge one's shadow—that dark, destructive underside of the personality that is repressed and then projected onto others. In midlife, Levin-son[4] found, "It is necessary that a man recognize and take responsi-bility for his own destructive capabilities." In the first half of his life, Lincoln cruelly belittled and satirized his political opponents, often wounding them deeply. After his midlife transition, he abandoned that practice. In 1864 he said, with much justice, "So long as I have been here [in Washington] I have not willingly planted a thorn in any man's bosom." Clearly, Lincoln came to terms with his destructive-ness between 1849 and 1854.

The psychological growth described here is not an act of will. The learning that takes place in a man's early forties is, according to Levinson, "not purely conscious or intellectual. It cannot be acquired simply by reading a few books, taking a few courses, or even having some psychotherapy . . . we often learn by going through intense periods of suffering, confusion, rage against others and ourselves, grief over lost opportunities and lost parts of the self."

After five years of such suffering, confusion, rage, and grief, Lin-coln emerged with what his law partner William Herndon called "that peculiar nature . . . which distinguishes one person from an-other, as much to say 'I am myself and not you.'" In 1859 an admirer noted that "what he [Lincoln] does & says is all his own. What Se-ward[5] and others do you feel that you have read in books or speeches, or that it is a sort of deduction from what the world is full of. But what Lincoln does you feel to be something newly mined

---

[4] Psychologist Daniel J. Levinson, in his book *The Season's of a Man's Life*, was the first to call the years 1849 to 1954 Lincoln's "midlife transition."

[5] Senator William Seward of New York became Lincoln's Secretary of State.

out—something above the ordinary." Although he remained ambitious, he no longer desperately needed collective approval. On September 30, 1863, he explained "with considerable feeling" to a group of Missourians, "It is my ambition and desire to so administer the affairs of the government while I remain president that if at the end I shall have lost every other friend on earth I shall at least have one friend remaining and that one shall be down inside of me." Nor did he lose his desire to be accommodating, but it was now tempered. In 1864 he told one of his secretaries that in dealing with congressional Radicals who opposed him on Reconstruction, "I must keep some consciousness of being somewhere near right: I must keep some standard of principle fixed within myself.". . .

Like anyone who has come to grips with his own shadow, Lincoln cherished no exalted self-image. "I am very sure," he told Noah Brooks[6] one day in the White House, "that if I do not go away from here a wiser man, I shall go away a better man, for having learned here what a very poor sort of a man I am." To a delegation of clergy, he declared, "I may not be a great man—(straightening up to his full height) I know I am not a great man." John Hay[7] was impressed by the difference between the president and the petty egomaniacs surrounding him. To his diary Hay confided on July 31, 1863, "While the rest are grinding their little private organs for their own glorification[,] the old man is working with the strength of a giant and the purity of an angel to do this great work."

Lincoln had so little egotism that even when he used the first-person singular pronoun it hardly seemed egocentric. James Russell Lowell,[8] commenting on Lincoln's "unconsciousness of self," noted that "he forgets himself so entirely in his object as to give his *I* the sympathetic and persuasive effect of *We* with the great body of his countrymen." This lack of egotism enabled Lincoln to relate to the people of the North, so that, in Lowell's words, "When he speaks, it seems as if the people were listening to their own thinking aloud." The rapport he enjoyed with the people allowed him to infuse his "unconquerable spirit" into them "in some mysterious manner," as Douglas Southall Freeman[9] put it.

Leo Tolstoy[10] detected a God-like quality in Lincoln. Admiring his "peculiar moral power" and "the greatness of his character," Tolstoy said, "He was what Beethoven was in music, Dante in poetry, Raphael in painting, and Christ in the philosophy of life. He aspired to be divine—and he was." Some of his constituents believed that if Lincoln were not divine, at least he had been placed in office to do

---

[6] Brooks, a friend, wrote a biography of Lincoln in 1888.
[7] Hay was one of Lincoln's two presidential secretaries.
[8] Lowell was a prominent New England poet.
[9] Freeman is author of *George Washington, A Biography.*
[10] Tolstoy was a Russian novelist and mystic.

the work of the Almighty. John Hay told his fellow White House secretary John G. Nicolay in the summer of 1863 that their boss "is in fine whack. I have rarely seen him more serene & busy. He is managing this war, the draft, foreign relations, and planning a reconstruction of the Union, all at once. . . . There is no man in the country, so wise, so gentle and so firm. I believe the hand of God placed him where he is." . . .

Lincoln's high degree of consciousness enabled him to suppress his own egotism while steadily focussing on the main goal: victory in the Civil War. As a friend observed, "He managed his politics upon a plan entirely different from any other man the country has ever produced. . . . In his conduct of the war he acted upon the theory that but one thing was necessary, and that was a united North. He had all shades of sentiments and opinions to deal with, and the consideration was always presented to his mind: How can I hold these discordant elements together? In a less conscious man, envy, jealousy, self-righteousness, false pride, vanity, and the other foibles of ordinary humanity would have undermined his ability to maintain Northern unity and resolve. That task required "utter forgetfulness of self," and such forgetfulness of self, the ability to overcome the petty tyranny of the ego, developed only after he had wrestled long and hard—and successfully—with the challenges of midlife.

THE ROAD TO THE WHITE HOUSE

During the period 1849 to 1854 Lincoln's mature personality was formed in the heat of a mid-life crisis. From 1855 to 1860 his mature political personality and philosophy were fashioned by a combination of early convictions, current events, and a desire, once more burning, to play a role in public affairs, and even national politics.

His Whig Party, the party of his hero, Henry Clay, was dying; as a political realist he knew it was time for a new party to rise in opposition to the majority Democrats, the descendants of Andrew Jackson. He became a founding member of the Republican Party, leading his local Illinois chapter and working to make one of the new party's major themes opposition to the extension of slavery into the newly created territories. He also worked to limit the influence in his party of the faction that came out of the old Know-Nothing Party, infamous for its opposition to immigration. A story he often related during those days was directed at the absurdity of this group's assumptions:

I had some time ago an Irishman named Patrick cultivating my garden. One morning I went out to see how he was getting along. "Mr. Lincoln, what do yez think of these Know-Nothings?" he inquired. I explained what they were trying to do, and asked Pat why he had not been born in America. "Faith," he replied, "I wanted to, but me mother wouldn't let me."

Lincoln was a valuable asset to the Republicans not only because he was a former congressman but because his logical mind helped formulate political positions and his constantly improving orational skills made him a crowd pleaser and vote getter. His stump delivery seemed stronger, more forceful, and more convincing by the month. Historian David Donald perhaps best describes Lincoln the speaker in the following paragraph about the first time Lincoln spoke on the same platform with Illinois Senator Stephen A. Douglas, whom in 1858 he would challenge for his seat in the U.S. Senate:

Before an audience described as "very large, intelligent, and attentive," Lincoln spoke for more than three hours. The afternoon was hot and sticky, and Lincoln, as though prepared for heavy physical labor, appeared in his shirtsleeves, without collar or tie. Unlike many the speakers, he did not pace back and forth on the platform or lean on the lectern; instead, as Herndon said, "he stood square on his feet, with both of his legs straight up and down, toe even with toe." As always, he was a little awkward at the outset, and initially his voice was "sharp—shrill piping and squeaky." Once he was under way, the pitch of his voice lowered and "became harmonious—melodious—musical." He nearly always held his hands behind his back when he began a speech, the left hand grasped in the palm of the right, but as he proceeded, would bring his hands forward, often holding the left lapel of his coat with his left hand while leaving the right hand free to emphasize his points. He did not gesture much with his hands, however, and mostly emphasized his points with a jerk and snap of his head. But occasionally he would stretch out his long right arm and his bony forefinger to drive an idea home, and at moments of great inspiration he would "raise both hands toward heaven at an angle of about 50 degrees, generally the palms up."

From all contemporary accounts, Lincoln was, despite a tenor voice and a thin but tall frame, a persuasive orator. Another student of his public speech has written:

Sitting on the platform, Lincoln was not an imposing figure. Slouched in a chair, his lean legs crossed, hands sometimes crammed in trouser pockets, he seemed no taller than the average man. But when he rose to speak, the audience was startled at the phenomenal change in appearance. His height of six feet four inches was majestic; his clear, high-pitched voice distinctly reached the outskirts of the biggest crowd; the deep-set eyes flashed and twinkled; the droll, captivating smile which expanded his furrowed cheeks revealed a mouth full of white, regular teeth, and wreathed his whole countenance in animation.

Sparing in the use of gestures, Lincoln stood squarely on his feet, with hands clasped behind his back, or one hand clutching the lapel of his coat and the other hanging easily at his side. When deeply moved, he would stretch himself beyond his already enormous height, throw his long, sinewy arms high above his head, pause for an instant in this attitude, and then sweep his huge fists through the air with a crashing emphasis that no one ever forgot.

A House Divided: 1858

An appropriate place to begin a study of the speeches containing the political philosophy and platform that would take Lincoln to the White House is his "House Divided" speech, delivered in his home town of Springfield on June 16, 1858. He was just beginning then to form his position on slavery as he opened his campaign to unseat Stephen A. Douglas and go himself to the U.S. Senate.

Mr. President and Gentlemen of the Convention. If we could first know where we are, and whither we are tending, we could better judge what to do, and how to do it. We are now far into the fifth year, since a policy was initiated with the avowed object, and confident promise, of putting an end to slavery agitation. Under the operation of that policy, that agitation[11] has not only not ceased, but has constantly augmented. In my opinion, it will not cease, until a crisis shall have been reached and passed. "A house divided against itself cannot stand."[12] I believe this government cannot endure permanently half slave and half free. I do not expect the Union to be dissolved—I do not expect the house to fall—but I do expect it will cease to be divided. It will become all one thing, or all the other. Either the opponents of slavery, will arrest the further spread of it, and place it where the public mind shall rest in the belief that it is in the

---

[11] Lincoln refers here to the Kansas-Nebraska Act, written by Senator Douglas, which prohibited slavery in Nebraska but permitted it in Kansas, a violation in Lincoln's view of the Missouri Compromise of 1829, which forever prohibited slavery north of 36'30", the southern border of Missouri.

[12] Lincoln is here loosely quoting Matthew 12:25, in which Jesus addressed critics who said that he cast out demons by the power of the Devil: "Every city or house divided against itself shall not stand."

course of ultimate extinction; or its advocates will push it forward, till
it shall become alike lawful in all the States, old as well as new—
North as well as South.

The Dred Scott decision, in which the U.S. Supreme Court said
a slave could not claim freedom even if he reached free soil, had
come down the year before. Douglas, Lincoln said, had defended
that decision, even though it meant to the nation the following:

First, That no negro slave, imported as such from Africa, and no de-
scendant of such slave, can ever be a citizen of any State, in the sense
of that term as used in the Constitution of the United States. This
point is made in order to deprive the negro, in every possible event,
of the benefit of that provision of the United States Constitution,
which declares that: "The citizens of each State shall be entitled to all
privileges and immunities of citizens in the several States."

Secondly, That "subject to the Constitution of the United
States," neither Congress nor a Territorial Legislature can exclude
slavery from any United States Territory. This point is made in order
that individual men may fill up the Territories with slaves, without
danger of losing them as property, and thus to enhance the chances
of permanency to the institution through all the future.

Thirdly, That whether the holding of a negro in actual slavery in
a free State, makes him free, as against the holder, the United States
courts will not decide, but will leave to be decided by the courts of
any slave State the negro may be forced into by the master. This
point is made, not to be pressed immediately; but, if acquiesced in
for a while, and apparently endorsed by the people at an election,
then to sustain the logical conclusion that what Dred Scott's master
might lawfully do with Dred Scott, in the free State of Illinois, every
other master may lawfully do with any other one, or one thousand
slaves, in Illinois, or in any other free State.

Auxiliary to all this, and working hand in hand with it, the Nebraska doctrine,[13] or what is left of it, is to educate and mould public opinion, at least Northern public opinion, not to care whether
slavery is voted down or voted up. This shows exactly where we now
are; and partially, also, whither we are tending.

Lincoln then explained that the nation was just one Supreme
Court decision away from making slavery legal in all states of the
Union. All it needed to do, in response to the right case, was declare that the Constitution did not permit a State to exclude slavery from its limits. He then concluded:

---

[13] One free state would be admitted to balance each slave state.

There are those who denounce us openly to their own friends, and yet whisper us softly, that Senator Douglas is the aptest instrument there is, with which to affect that object. They wish us to *infer* all, from the facts, that he now has a little quarrel with the present head of the dynasty; and that he has regularly voted with us, on a single point, upon which, he and we, have never differed. They remind us that he is a very great man, and that the largest of us are very small ones. Let this be granted. But "a living dog is better than a dead lion." Judge Douglas, if not a dead lion for his work, is at least a caged and toothless one. How can he oppose the advances of slavery? He don't care anything about it. His avowed mission is impressing the "public heart" to *care nothing about* it. A leading Douglas Democratic newspaper thinks Douglas' superior talent will be needed to resist the revival of the African slave trade. Does Douglas believe an effort to revive that trade is approaching? He has not said so. Does he really think so? But if it is, how can he resist it? For years he has labored to prove it a sacred right of white men to take negro slaves into the new territories. Can he possibly show that it is less a sacred right to buy them where they can be bought cheapest? And unquestionably they can be bought cheaper in Africa than in Virginia. He has done all in his power to reduce the whole question of slavery to one of a mere right of property; and as such, how can he oppose the foreign slave trade—how can he refuse that trade in that "property" shall be "perfectly free"—unless he does it as a protection to the home production? And as the home producers will probably not ask the protection, he will be wholly without a ground of opposition.

Senator Douglas holds, we know, that a man may rightfully be wiser to-day than he was yesterday—that he may rightfully change when he finds himself wrong. But, can we for that reason, run ahead, and infer that he will make any particular change, of which he, himself, has given no intimation? Can we safely base our action upon any such vague inference? Now, as ever, I wish not to misrepresent Judge Douglas' position, question his motives, or do aught that can be personally offensive to him. Whenever, if ever, he and we can come together on principle so that our cause may have assistance from his great ability, I hope to have interposed no adventitious obstacle. But clearly, he is not now with us—he does not pretend to be—he does not promise ever to be.

Our cause, then, must be intrusted to, and conducted by, its own undoubted friends—those whose hands are free, whose hearts are in the work—who *do care* for the result. Two years ago the Republicans of the nation mustered over thirteen hundred thousand strong. We did this under the single impulse of resistance to a common danger, with every external circumstance against us. Of strange, discordant, and even hostile elements, we gathered from the four winds, and formed and fought the battle through, under the constant hot fire of a disciplined, proud and pampered enemy. Did we brave all them to falter now?—now, when the same enemy is wavering, dissevered and belligerent? The result is not doubtful. We shall not fail—if we stand firm, we *shall not fail.* Wise counsels may accelerate, or mistakes delay it, but, sooner or later, the victory is sure to come.

Debating Douglas: 1858

Lincoln was nominated by the Republicans to oppose Democrat Douglas's reelection to the Senate. Since senators were not then elected by popular vote, the Illinois House elected that November would choose the next Senator. Thus, Lincoln's main objectives were to focus on the issues, give voters a choice, and help assure a Republican legislative majority. Gambling that Douglas's vanity would prevent him from rejecting a challenge, he offered to debate him in cities in seven parts of the state and was rewarded when Douglas accepted.

Beginning August 12 in Ottawa, the debates moved to Freeport in the northwest corner of the state, then to Jonesboro, which though in a free state lies on a line south of Richmond, Virginia. Then they debated through September and October in Charleston, Galesburg, Quincy, and finally before a crowd of 6,000 at Alton. Using a newly devised shorthand, reporters captured and published "verbatim" accounts of the debates, although reporters of the two persuasions cast their accounts of the debates, the effectiveness of the debates, and crowd reactions in widely different forms.

The Lincoln biographer who has best captured the flavor and significance of the debates is poet Carl Sandburg in his *Abraham Lincoln: The Prairie Years.* Sandburg, born on the American plains to illiterate parents who had immigrated from Sweden, is one of the least objective but most verbally gifted of Lincoln's biographers.

> Two men had spoken in Illinois to audiences surpassing any in past American history in size and in eagerness to hear. Yet they also spoke to the nation. The main points of the debates reached millions of readers. Newspapers in the larger cities printed the reports in full. A book of passion, an almanac of American visions, victories, defeats, a catechism of national thought and hope, were in the paragraphs of the debates. A powerful fragment of America breathed in Douglas' saying at Quincy: "Let each State mind its own business and let its neighbors alone! . . . If we will stand by that principle, then Mr. Lincoln will find that this republic can exist forever divided into free and

slave States . . . Stand by that great principle and we can go on as we have done, increasing in wealth, in population, in power, and in all the elements of greatness, until we shall be the admiration and terror of the world, . . . until we make this continent one ocean-bound republic."

Those who wished quiet about the slavery question, and those who didn't, understood Lincoln's inquiry: "You say it [slavery] is wrong; but don't you constantly . . . argue that this is not the right place to oppose it? You say it must not be opposed in the free States, because slavery is not here; it must not be opposed in the slave States, because it is there; it must not be opposed in politics, because that will make a fuss; it must not be opposed in the pulpit, because it is not religion. Then where is the place to oppose it? There is no suitable place to oppose it."

So many could respond to the Lincoln view: "Judge Douglas will have it that I want a negro wife. He never can be brought to understand that there is any middle ground on this subject. I have lived until my fiftieth year, and have never had a negro woman either for a slave or a wife, and I think I can live fifty centuries, for that matter, without having had one for either." Pointing to the Supreme Court decision that slaves as property could not be voted out of new territories, Lincoln said, "His [Douglas'] Supreme Court cooperating with him, has *squatted* his Squatter Sovereignty out." The argument had got down as thin as "soup made by boiling the shadow of a pigeon that had starved to death."

Douglas said he would not be brutal. "Humanity requires, and Christianity commands that you shall extend to every inferior being, and every dependent being, all the privileges, immunities and advantages which can be granted to them consistent with the safety of society." America was a young and growing nation. "It swarms as often as a hive of bees . . . In less than fifteen years, if the same progress that has distinguished this country for the last fifteen years continues, every foot of vacant land between this and the Pacific ocean, owned by the United States, will be occupied . . . And just as fast as our interests and our destiny require additional territory in the north, in the south, or on the islands of the ocean, I am for it, and when we acquire it will leave the people, ... free to do as they please on the subject of slavery and every other question."

Lincoln cited a Supreme Court decision as "one of the thousand things constantly done to prepare the public mind to make property, and nothing but property, of the negro in all the states of this Union." Why was slavery referred to in "covert language" and not mentioned plainly and openly in the U.S. Constitution? Why were the words "negro" and "slavery" left out? Was it not always the single issue of quarrels? "Does it not enter into the churches and rend them asunder? What divided the great Methodist Church into two parts, North and South? What has raised this constant disturbance in every Presbyterian General Assembly that meets?" It was not politicians; this fact and issue of slavery operated on the minds of men and divided them in every avenue of society, in politics, religion, literature, morals. "That is the issue that will continue in this country when these poor tongues of Judge Douglas and myself shall be silent. It is the eternal struggle between these two principles . . . The one is the common right of humanity and the other the divine right of kings. It is the same . . . spirit that says, 'You work and toil and earn bread, and I'll eat it.' No matter in what shape it comes, whether from the mouth of a king who seeks to bestride the people of his own nation and live by the fruit of their labor, or from one race of men as an apology for enslaving another race, it is the same tyrannical principle."

At Freeport Lincoln put a series of questions to Douglas, one of them, "Can the people of a United States Territory, in any lawful way, against the wish of any citizen of the United States, exclude slavery from its limits prior to the formation of a State Constitution?" The answer of Douglas amounted to saying, "Yes." It raised a storm of opposition to him in the South, and lost him big blocks of northern Democratic friends who wanted to maintain connections in the South.

When Douglas twisted his antislavery position into one of race quality, Lincoln replied it was an arrangement of words by which a man can prove a horse chestnut to be a chestnut horse. At Charleston he shook a finger at a man's face: "I assert that you are here to-day, and you undertake to prove me a liar by showing that you were in Mattoon yesterday. I say that you took your hat off your head, and you prove me a liar by putting it on your head. That is the whole force of Douglas' argument."

Of Lincoln's face in a hotel room in Quincy, David R. Locke wrote: "I never saw a more thoughtful face. I never saw a more dignified face. I never saw so sad a face."

Yet given Lincoln's irrepressible wit, the debates were not without humor. Anthony Gross recounts this funny exchange:

> On another occasion Douglas, in one of his speeches, made a strong point against Lincoln by telling the crowd that when he first knew Mr. Lincoln he was a "grocery-keeper," and sold whisky, cigars, etc. "Mr. L.," he said, "was a very good bartender!" This brought the laugh on Lincoln, whose reply, however, soon came, and then the laugh was on the other side.
>
> "What Mr. Douglas has said, gentlemen," replied Lincoln, "is true enough; I did keep a grocery, and I did sell cotton, candles and cigars, and sometimes whisky; but I remember in those days that Mr. Douglas was one of my best customers. Many a time have I stood on one side of the counter and sold whisky to Mr. Douglas on the other

side, but the difference between us now is this: I have left my side of
the counter, but Mr. Douglas still sticks to his as tenaciously as ever."

On election day, November 2, Lincoln out-polled Douglas by
4,085 votes in a nonbinding popular tally. Republican candidates
for the legislature got 50 percent of the popular vote to 48 percent for the Democrats, but Democrats won 54 seats to the Republicans' 46. Lincoln could not be elected to the United States
Senate. He was not surprised by the results, but he was bitterly
disappointed. He had exerted enormous energy and lost, but he
tried to make the most of it: "Though I now sink out of view, and
shall be forgotten, I believe I have made some marks which will
tell for the cause of civil liberty long after I am gone." Then he
joked that he felt like the boy who stubbed his toe: "It hurt too
hard to laugh, and he was too big to cry."

On January 5, 1859, the new legislature elected Douglas 54 to
46. Lincoln told a friend: "The fight must go on. The cause of civil
liberty must not be surrendered at the end of one or even one
hundred defeats." According to Sandburg, that night as he walked
home he almost took a fall on the slick street, but he caught himself in time. "It's a slip, not a fall," he said, then laughed and repeated the meaningful phrase.

Cooper Union Address: 1860

Indeed, for Lincoln's career the defeat in 1858–59 was not a fall.
It was actually not even a slip. Newspaper accounts of his debate
with Douglas made him a nationally known and throughout the
North a respected figure. He was by 1860 in a position to be nominated Republican candidate for president of the United States.

On February 27, 1860, he addressed the Cooper Union forum
in the city of New York. Founded just the year before by wealthy in-
vestor Peter Cooper, the Union was dedicated to education and
public issues. Lincoln's invitation to speak there demonstrated how
seriously he was being taken in the East, and his ready acceptance
of the invitation, along with the thorough way he prepared his statement on slavery, demonstrated how much he wanted the presidential nomination. It is clear from his words that his public philosophy
had grown to the standards of a candidate for president, the nation's highest office, at the moment of the nation's greatest crisis.

Abe Lincoln as he traveled the country making speeches in 1859–60, working to become the Republican Party's nominee for President of the United States.

Lincoln began by quoting Senator Douglas from a speech he had given in Columbus, Ohio: "Our fathers, when they framed the Government under which we live, understood this question just as well, and even better, than we do now." Then he asked the question, What was the understanding of those fathers?, and he answered, in the first half of the speech, that the founding fathers did not foresee the extension of slavery to any new territories. Indeed, under the leadership of George Washington, Congress had specifically prohibited its extension into the old Northwest. While Lincoln was not prepared to argue that slavery was unconstitutional, he was saying without equivocation that it should not be taken to the western lands.

After denying to the general public that Republicans were abolitionists, radicals, or in any way responsible for John Brown's capture of the Harpers Ferry arsenal the previous year, he addressed his Republican Party:

A few words now to Republicans. It is exceedingly desirable that all parts of this great Confederacy shall be at peace, and in harmony, one with another. Let us Republicans do our part to have it so. Even though much provoked, let us do nothing through passion and ill temper. Even though the southern people will not so much as listen to us, let us calmly consider their demands, and yield to them if, in our deliberate view of our duty, we possibly can. Judging by all they say and do, and by the subject and nature of their controversy with us, let us determine, if we can, what will satisfy them.

Will they be satisfied if the Territories be unconditionally surrendered to them? We know they will not. In all their present complaints against us, the Territories are scarcely mentioned. Invasions and insurrections are the rage now. Will it satisfy them, if, in the future, we have nothing to do with invasions and insurrections? We know it will not. We so know, because we know we never had anything to do with invasions and insurrections; and yet this total abstaining does not exempt us from the charge and the denunciation.

The question recurs, what will satisfy them? Simply this: We must not only let them alone, but we must, somehow, convince them that we do let them alone. This, we know by experience, is no easy task. We have been so trying to convince them from the very beginning of our organization, but with no success. In all our platforms and speeches we have constantly protested our purpose to let them alone; but this has had no tendency to convince them. Alike unavailing to convince them, is the fact that they have never detected a man of us in any attempt to disturb them.

These natural, and apparently adequate means all failing, what will convince them? This, and this only: cease to call slavery wrong, and join them in calling it *right*. And this must be done thoroughly—done in acts as well as in words. Silence will not be tolerated—we must place ourselves avowedly with them. Senator Douglas's new sedition law must be enacted and enforced, suppressing all declarations that slavery is wrong, whether made in politics, in presses, in pulpits, or in private. We must arrest and return their fugitive slaves with greedy pleasure. We must pull down our Free State constitutions. The whole atmosphere must be disinfected from all taint of opposition to slavery, before they will cease to believe that all their troubles proceed from us.

I am quite aware they do not state their case precisely in this way. Most of them would probably say to us, "Let us alone, *do* nothing to us, and say what you please about slavery." But we do let them alone—have never disturbed them—so that, after all, it is what we say, which dissatisfies them. They will continue to accuse us of doing, until we cease saying.

I am also aware they have not, as yet, in terms, demanded the overthrow of our Free-State Constitutions. Yet those Constitutions declare the wrong of slavery, with more solemn emphasis, than do all other sayings against it; and when all these other sayings have been silenced, the overthrow of these Constitutions will be demanded, and nothing be left to resist the demand. It is nothing to the contrary, that they do not demand the whole of this just now. Demanding what they do, and for the reason they do, they can voluntarily stop nowhere short of this consummation. Holding, as they do, that slavery is morally right, and socially elevating, they cannot cease to demand a full national recognition of it, as a legal right, and a social blessing.

Nor can we justifiably withhold this, on any ground save our conviction that slavery is wrong. If slavery is right, all words, acts, laws, and constitutions against it, are themselves wrong, and should be silenced, and swept away. If it is right, we cannot justly object to its nationality—its universality; if it is wrong, they cannot justly insist upon its extension—its enlargement. All they ask, we could readily grant, if we thought slavery right; all we ask, they could as readily grant, if they thought it wrong. Their thinking it right, and our thinking it wrong, is the precise fact upon which depends the whole controversy. Thinking it right, as they do, they are not to blame for desiring its full recognition, as being right; but, thinking it wrong, as we do, can we yield to them? Can we cast our votes with their view, and against our own? In view of our moral, social, and political responsibilities, can we do this?

Wrong as we think slavery is, we can yet afford to let it alone where it is, because that much is due to the necessity arising from its actual presence in the nation; but can we, while our votes will prevent it, allow it to spread into the National Territories, and to overrun us here in these Free States? If our sense of duty forbids this, then let us stand by our duty, fearlessly and effectively. Let us be diverted by none of those sophistical contrivances wherewith we are so industriously plied and belabored—contrivances such as groping for some middle ground between the right and the wrong, vain as the search for a man who should be neither a living man nor a dead man—such as a policy of "don't care" on a question about which all true men do care—such as Union appeals beseeching true Union men to yield to Disunionists, reversing the divine rule, and calling, not the sinners, but the righteous to repentance—such as invocations to Washington, imploring men to unsay what Washington said, and undo what Washington did.

Neither let us be slandered from our duty by false accusations against us, nor frightened from it by menaces of destruction to the Government nor of dungeons to ourselves. LET US HAVE FAITH THAT RIGHT MAKES MIGHT, AND IN THAT FAITH, LET US, TO THE END, DARE TO DO OUR DUTY AS WE UNDERSTAND IT.

SUMMARY: GROWTH AND OPPORTUNITY

In 1850, when Lincoln was forty-one, there was little to predict that he would become president of the United States, and certainly not a great president. If anything, people who knew him would have expected little more than a measure of material comfort to come from his law practice, the only career seemingly left to him. Born of poor agrarian stock, with almost no formal education, self-taught but not thoroughly well-read in the law, he had been an undistinguished state legislator and self-confessed failure as a U.S. congressman. His marriage was a trial, his wife often unhappy with him, and his second son had just died. He was given to fits of despondency that might lead to permanent mental disability. Yet Lincoln put aside his personal troubles, shook off his public shortcomings, and grew in the space of a decade to become the man a nation in crisis chose, at the age of fifty-one, to lead it through its darkest hour. Events conspired to offer him a prominent role to play: the issue of slavery in the western territories, the Kansas-Nebraska Act, the Dred Scott decision, John Brown's attack upon the Harpers Ferry arsenal. All of which drove a wedge deeply into the age-old division between North and South, leading to a crisis in which only a candidate who refused to compromise could win, taking the Northern and sacrificing the Southern vote. But Lincoln was himself the key to his own success. Strong convictions enabled him to use his native gifts, to grow into the man who could take advantage of the opportunities about to present themselves, to be elected president, and to achieve greatness.

QUESTIONS FOR RESPONSIVE ESSAYS

1. How did Lincoln's humble birth, early poverty, and lack of formal education mold him into the man he became? Was he stronger because of them, or would someone of his natural talents have been stronger with more material advantages?

2. In what ways did Lincoln's marriage to Mary Todd contribute to his career? Did she inspire him to greatness, or did he have to

ignore her in order to achieve his goals? What part did his sons play in his career?

3. What part did Lincoln's physical appearance and the way his mind worked help or hinder him in his practice of law and political career? How did they contribute to his success as a political orator?

4. Do you agree or disagree with Michael Burlingame that Lincoln had a mid-life crisis that led to his maturation and "individuation"? How does a psychohistorical analysis like Burlingame's help to explain a man like Lincoln, and how can it go too far in speculating about a person's inner self?

5. Describe Lincoln's famous gift for words and oral metaphor as shown by the speeches leading up to his nomination for president. How did he mold his frontier speech to address the great issues of the day and prove himself capable of solving them?

A Lincoln

PART II

Lincoln the President

Had Abraham Lincoln not been elected president of the United States, he would today be a footnote in American history. He would be remembered as Douglas's opponent in the 1858 Senate race, a man who helped clarify the issues that led to Civil War. He might have become a senator himself after winning a future race, since Douglas died before the next one. He might have served in the cabinet of a Republican president, perhaps Seward or Frémont, or been appointed military governor of a territory or conquered Southern state during the war. Or perhaps there would never have been a war, if Lincoln or the Republicans had not won in 1860.

A unique combination of events allowed Lincoln to become the sixteenth president of the United States. His debates with Douglas spread his name across the nation and gave him a specific public identity. His modest background, western frontier image, oratorical skills, and firm but moderate convictions made the Republican Party choose him as its standard-bearer over other possible candidates, some better educated and more sophisticated, some better positioned to win the more populated eastern states, some more radically dedicated to the abolition of slavery. The fact that the Democrats, then the majority party in the United States, split into northern and southern branches, each with a nominee, allowed Lincoln to win a solid majority of electoral votes while winning barely 40 percent of the popular vote.

Lincoln's election led directly to the secession from the Union of eleven Southern states, none of which he carried, and thus to the Civil War. The war, which effectively ended the first phase of

U.S. history and initiated a second, was pivotal in the development of the American nation. Lincoln, who was president exactly the length of the war, became a creator of the American mind. It is impossible to imagine modern America without President Abraham Lincoln.

THE ELECTION OF 1860

Lincoln was elected president long before the days of modern campaigning. He did not appear at the Chicago convention to give an acceptance speech when he was nominated. A delegation from the convention visited him in Springfield to inform him of his nomination, although he of course had already heard the news. He did not travel the country looking for votes but rather hosted delegations and made a few speeches at his home. Election night saw him not at a victory party but reading telegraph messages in Springfield.

The majority Democratic Party nominated Stephen Douglas, but a Southern faction met later and nominated John C. Breckinridge of Kentucky, an act which led to a splintering of the Democratic vote. To complicate things even more, a Constitutional Union Party nominated John Bell of Tennessee. Lincoln won only 39.8 percent of the popular vote. He failed to carry a single Southern or border state but he carried all of the populous northeastern and northwestern states and won a majority 180 electoral votes, which assured his victory, although it was decidedly regional. Douglas won 29.5 percent of the popular vote but only two border states and 12 electoral votes. Breckinridge won 18.1 percent of the popular vote and 72 electoral votes, carrying the entire deep South. Bell won 12.6 percent of the vote, three border states, and 39 electoral votes.

The election convinced Southerners that the Union was irretrievably divided and that their enemy would be in the White House the next spring. Secession began. Secession led to war.

LEAVING SPRINGFIELD

On February 11, 1861, the day before his fifty-second birthday and three weeks before he would be inaugurated as president, Lincoln boarded a train for the journey east to take office amid a national crisis. The words he spoke to his fellow citizens in Springfield revealed how aware he was of the dangers he faced—for the nation, for himself.

> My Friends:
>   No one, not in my situation, can appreciate my feeling of sadness at this parting. To this place, and the kindness of these people, I owe everything. Here I have lived a quarter of a century, and have passed from a young to an old man. Here my children have been born, and one is buried. I now leave, not knowing when or whether ever I may return, with a task before me greater than that which rested upon Washington. Without the assistance of that Divine Being who ever attended him, I cannot succeed. With that assistance, I cannot fail. Trusting in Him who can go with me, and remain with you, and be everywhere for good, let us confidently hope that all will yet be well. To His care commending you, as I hope in your prayers you will commend me, I bid you an affectionate farewell.

He said he did not know whether he would return—and indeed he did not, except on his funeral train. He said his task was greater than that of the first president, George Washington—and it was. He mentioned God and God's aid four times, something he had not done during his years of seeking office—but he was now to be president, and one of his roles was to be the priest of America's "political religion." More of that later.

THE FIRST INAUGURAL ADDRESS: 1861

Times were uncertain and conditions so insecure that, although he was well-received throughout his Northern journey, the president-elect had to be brought through Southern-leaning Maryland and into the District of Columbia secretly. Before his inauguration on March 4, 1861, seven Southern states had seceded from the Union, and shortly after he became president four others followed them, with three more threatening. Thus Lincoln's inaugural address, by its timing, was one of the most significant speeches in American history. Lincoln had made clear in previous addresses his opposition to the extension of slavery and his complete commitment to preserving the Union. Now as president he gave these convictions authority.

Fellow citizens of the United States:

In compliance with a custom as old as the government itself, I appear before you to address you briefly, and to take, in your presence, the oath prescribed by the Constitution of the United States, to be taken by the President "before he enters on the execution of his office."

I do not consider it necessary, at present, for me to discuss those matters of administration about which there is no special anxiety, or excitement.

Apprehension seems to exist among the people of the Southern States, that by the accession of a Republican Administration, their property, and their peace, and personal security, are to be endangered. There has never been any reasonable cause for such apprehension. Indeed, the most ample evidence to the contrary has all the while existed, and been open to their inspection. It is found in nearly all the published speeches of him who now addresses you. I do but quote from one of those speeches when I declare that "I have no purpose, directly or indirectly, to interfere with the institution of slavery in the States where it exists. I believe I have no lawful right to do so, and I have no inclination to do so." Those who nominated and elected me did so with full knowledge that I had made this, and many similar declarations, and had never recanted them. And more than this, they placed in the platform, for my acceptance, and as a law to themselves, and to me, the clear and emphatic resolution which I now read:

"Resolved, That the maintenance inviolate of the rights of the States, and especially the right of each State to order and control its own domestic institutions according to its own judgment exclusively, is essential to that balance of power on which the perfection and endurance of our political fabric depend; and we denounce the lawless invasion by armed force of the soil of any State or Territory, no matter under what pretext, as among the gravest of crimes."

I now reiterate these sentiments: and in doing so, I only press upon the public attention the most conclusive evidence of which the case is susceptible, that the property, peace and security of no section are to be in anywise endangered by the now incoming Administration. I add too, that all the protection which, consistently with the Constitution and the laws, can be given, will be cheerfully given to all the States when lawfully demanded, for whatever cause—as cheerfully to one section, as to another. . . .

It is seventy-two years since the first inauguration of a President under our national Constitution. During that period fifteen different and greatly distinguished citizens, have, in succession, administered the executive branch of the government. They have conducted it through many perils; and, generally, with great success. Yet, with all this scope for precedent, I now enter upon the same task for the brief constitutional term of four years, under great and peculiar difficulty.

A disruption of the Federal Union heretofore only menaced, is now formidably attempted.

I hold, that in contemplation of universal law, and of the Constitution, the Union of these States is perpetual. Perpetuity is implied, if not expressed, in the fundamental law of all national governments. It is safe to assert that no government proper, ever had a provision in its organic law for its own termination. Continue to execute all the express provisions of our national Constitution, and the Union will endure forever—it being impossible to destroy it, except by some action not provided for in the instrument itself.

Again, if the United States be not a government proper, but an association of States in the nature of contract merely, can it, as a contract, be peaceably unmade, by less than all the parties who made it? One party to a contract may violate it—break it, so to speak; but does it not require all to lawfully rescind it?

Descending from these general principles, we find the proposition that, in legal contemplation, the Union is perpetual, confirmed by the history of the Union itself. The Union is much older than the Constitution. It was formed in fact, by the Articles of Association in 1774. It was matured and continued by the Declaration of Independence in 1776. It was further matured and the faith of all the then thirteen States expressly plighted and engaged that it should be perpetual, by the Articles of Confederation in 1778. And finally, in 1787, one of the declared objects for ordaining and establishing the Constitution, was "*to form a more perfect union.*"

But if destruction of the Union, by one, or by a part only, of the States, be lawfully possible, the Union is *less* perfect than before the Constitution, having lost the vital element of perpetuity.

It follows from these views that no State, upon its own mere motion, can lawfully get out of the Union,—that *resolves* and *ordinances* to that effect are legally void; and that acts of violence, within any State or States, against the authority of the United States, are insurrectionary or revolutionary, according to the circumstances.

I therefore consider that, in view of the Constitution and the laws, the Union is unbroken; and, to the extent of my ability, I shall take care, as the Constitution itself expressly enjoins upon me, that the laws of the Union be faithfully executed in all the States. Doing this I deem to be only a simple duty on my part; and I shall perform it, so far as practicable, unless my rightful masters, the American people, shall withhold the requisite means, or, in some authoritative manner, direct the contrary. I trust this will not be regarded as a menace, but only as the declared purpose of the Union that it will constitutionally defend, and maintain itself.

In doing this there needs to be no bloodshed or violence; and there shall be none, unless it be forced upon the national authority. . . .

One section of our country believes slavery is *right,* and ought to be extended, while the other believes it is *wrong,* and ought not be extended. This is the only substantial dispute. The fugitive slave clause of the Constitution, and the law for the suppression of the foreign slave trade, are each as well enforced, perhaps, as *any* law can ever be in a community where the moral sense of the people imperfectly supports the law itself. The great body of the people abide by the dry legal obligation in both cases, and a few break over in each. This, I think, cannot be perfectly cured; and it would be worse in both cases *after* the separation of the sections, than before. The foreign slave trade, now imperfectly suppressed, would be ultimately revived without restriction, in one section; while fugitive slaves, now only partially surrendered, would not be surrendered at all, by the other.

Physically speaking, we cannot separate. We cannot remove our respective sections from each other, nor build an impassable wall between them. A husband and wife may be divorced, and go out of the presence, and beyond the reach of each other; but the different parts of our country cannot do this. They cannot but remain face to face; and intercourse, either amicable or hostile, must continue between them. Is it possible then to make that intercourse more advantageous, or more satisfactory *after* separation than *before?* Can aliens make treaties easier than friends can make laws? Can treaties be more faithfully enforced between aliens, than laws can among friends? Suppose you go to war, you cannot fight always; and when, after much loss on both sides, and no gain on either, you cease fighting, the identical old questions, as to terms of intercourse, are again upon you. . . .

My countrymen, one and all, think calmly and *well,* upon this whole subject. Nothing valuable can be lost by taking time. If there be an object to *hurry* any of you, in hot haste, to a step which you would never take *deliberately,* that object will be frustrated by taking time; but no good object can be frustrated by it. Such of you as are now dissatisfied, still have the old Constitution unimpaired, and, on the sensitive point, the laws of your own framing under it; while the new administration will have no immediate power, if it would, to change either. If it were admitted that you who are dissatisfied, hold the right side in the dispute, there still is no single good reason for precipitate action. Intelligence, patriotism, Christianity, and a firm reliance on Him, who has never yet forsaken this favored land, are still competent to adjust, in the best way, all our present difficulty.

In *your* hands, my dissatisfied fellow countrymen, and not in *mine,* is the momentous issue of civil war. The government will not assail *you.* You can have no conflict, without being yourself the aggressors. You have no oath registered in Heaven to destroy the government, while *I* shall have the most solemn one to "preserve, protect and defend" it.

I am loth to close. We are not enemies, but friends. We must not be enemies. Though passion may have strained, it must not

break our bonds of affection. <u>The mystic chords of memory, stretching from every battle-field, and patriot grave, to every living heart
and hearthstone, all over this broad land, will yet swell the chorus of
the Union, when again touched, as surely they will be, by the better
angels of our nature.</u>

PRESIDENT ABRAHAM LINCOLN

Lincoln looked and acted like no president before him. Having read
William Herndon's prosaic account of Lincoln's physical appearance, we might now consider Carl Sandburg's poetic description of
the newly elected president.

Lincoln was 51 years old. With each year since he had become a
grown man, his name and ways, and stories about him, had been
spreading among plain people and their children. So tall and so bony,
with so peculiar a slouch and so easy a saunter, so sad and so haunted-
looking, so quizzical and comic, as if hiding a lantern that lighted and
went out and that he lighted again—he was the Strange Friend and
the Friendly Stranger. Like something out of a picture book for children—he was. His form of slumping arches and his face of gaunt sock-
ets were a shape a Great Artist had scrawled from careless clay.

He looked like an original plan for an extra-long horse or a lean
tawny buffalo, that a Changer had suddenly whisked into a man-
shape. Or he met the eye as a clumsy, mystical giant that had walked
out of a Chinese or Russian fairy story, or a bogy who had stumbled
out of an ancient Saxon myth with a handkerchief full of presents he
wanted to divide among all the children in the world.

He didn't wear clothes. Rather, clothes hung upon him as if on
a rack to dry, or on a loose ladder up a windswept chimney. His
clothes, to keep the chill or the sun off, seemed to whisper, "He put
us on when he was thinking about something else."

He dressed any which way at times, in broadcloth, a silk hat, a
silk choker, and a flaming red silk handkerchief, so that one court
clerk said Lincoln was "fashionably dressed, as neatly attired as any
lawyer at court, except Ward Lamon." Or again, people said Lincoln
looked like a huge skeleton with skin over the bones, and clothes
covering the skin.

The stovepipe hat he wore sort of whistled softly: "I am not a
hat at all; I am the little garret roof where he tucks in little thoughts
he writes on pieces of paper." That hat, size seven and one-eighth,
had a brim one and three-quarters inches wide. The inside band in
which the more important letters and notes were tucked, measured
two and three-quarters inches. The cylinder of the stovepipe was 22
inches in circumference. The hat was lined with heavy silk and, measured inside, exactly six inches deep. And people tried to guess what

was going on under that hat. Written in pencil on the imitation satin paper that formed part of the lining was the signature "A. Lincoln, Springfield, Ill.," so that any forgetful person who might take the hat by mistake would know where to bring it back. Also the hatmaker, "George Hall, Springfield, Ill.," had printed his name in the hat so that Lincoln would know where to get another one just like it.

The umbrella with the name "Abraham Lincoln" stitched in, faded and drab from many rains and regular travels, looked sleepy and murmuring. "Sometime we shall have all the sleep we want; we shall turn the law office over to the spiders and the cobwebs; and we shall quit politics for keeps."

There could have been times when children and dreamers looked at Abraham Lincoln and lazily drew their eyelids half shut and let their hearts roam about him—and they half-believed him to be a tall horse chestnut tree or a rangy horse or a big wagon or a log barn full of new-mown hay—something else or more than a man, a lawyer, a Republican candidate with principles, a prominent citizen—something spreading, elusive, and mysterious—the Strange Friend and the Friendly Stranger.

The year of the big debates a boy had called out, "There goes old Mr. Lincoln," and Lincoln hearing it, remarked to a friend, "They commenced it when I was scarcely thirty years old." Often when people called him "Old Abe" they meant he had the texture and quaint friendliness of old handmade Bibles, old calfskin law books, weather-beaten oak and walnut planks, or wagon axles always willing in storm or stars.

More even than his appearance, it was Lincoln's humor that made him so different from his generally dour predecessors. While he took seriously his duties as president, especially in time of war, while he still occasionally fell into fits of gloom, he used humor to lighten his own burden and those of his colleagues. Anthony Gross captured many of Lincoln's witty stories and comments in his book *Lincoln's Own Stories*.

The following, for example, illustrates his impatience with verbosity:

> Robert Dale Owen, the spiritualist, once read the President a long manuscript on an abstruse subject with which that rather erratic person loved to deal. Lincoln listened patiently until the author asked for his opinion, when he replied with a yawn:
> "Well for those who like that sort of thing I should think it is just about the sort of thing they would like."

Another anecdote shows his lack of pretension even though he was president:

Senator Charles Sumner of Massachusetts called at the White House early one morning. He was told that the President was down-stairs, that he could go right down. He found the President polishing his boots. Somewhat amazed, Senator Sumner said, "Why, Mr. President, do you black your own boots?" With a vigorous rub of the brush, the President replied, "Whose boots did you think I blacked?"

He gave the following reply to a man who asked him for a pass through Federal troop lines in order to visit Richmond:

"I should be very happy to oblige you," said the President, "if my passes were respected; but the fact is, within the past two years I have given passes to Richmond to two hundred and fifty thousand men, and not one has got there yet."

He even handled the war and the fateful decisions he had to make about it with humor:

Some enemies and critics of General Grant once called upon Mr. Lincoln and urged him to oust Grant from his command. They repeated with malicious intent the gossip that Grant drank. "What does he drink?" asked Lincoln. "Whisky," was the answer, "and in unusual quantities." "Well," said the President, "just find out what particular kind he uses, and I'll send a barrel to each of the other generals."

He also reached for humor when newspapers began editorializing that since he had failed in four years to win the war he should not be elected to a second term. In response, Lincoln offered the following story:

A traveler on the frontier found himself out of his reckoning one night in a most inhospitable region. A terrific thunder-storm came up to add to his trouble. He floundered along until his horse at length gave out. The lightning afforded him the only clue to his way, but the peals of thunder were frightful. One bolt, which seemed to crash the earth beneath him, brought him to his knees. By no means a praying man, his petition was short and to the point: "O Lord, if it is all the same to you, give us a little *more light and a little less noise!*"

A MORE PERFECT UNION: THE GETTYSBURG ADDRESS

Upon assuming the presidency, Lincoln faced war. He spent his entire time as president fighting it. He did so, he explained, in order to preserve the Union, which was threatened by Southern secession. He had been elected to do this, and he would do so. He said so unequivocally in his first inaugural, and he emphasized it in nearly every presidential address. Speaking to a delegation of bank presidents who urged him to give up trying to keep the South and let the Union divide, he said:

> When I was a young man in Illinois I boarded for a time with the deacon of the Presbyterian church. One night I was roused from my sleep by a rap at the door, and I heard the deacon's voice exclaiming, "Arise, Abraham! The Day of Judgment has come!" I sprang from my bed and rushed to my window, and saw stars falling in great showers; but, looking back of them in the heavens, I saw the grand old constellations, with which I was so well acquainted, fixed and true in their places. Gentlemen, the world did not come to an end then, nor will the Union now.

At times, despite his vision of the Union, he changed directions and seemed not to steer a steady course. To explain his deviations, he told the story of a farm boy whose father told him to plow a straight furrow by heading toward a yoke of oxen on the opposite side of the field. The father left, and the boy began; but the oxen started to move, and when the father returned the boy had furrowed a circle instead of a line. Still he had reached the oxen, his goal.

Lincoln reached his goal and preserved the Union, but it took four long, destructive years, and it led him to emancipate the slaves (which he at first had been loath to do) and completely change the nation. The Union Lincoln left was strikingly different from the one that preceded him. It was perhaps also different from the one he had hoped to preserve.

On November 19, 1863, Lincoln delivered his most famous and philosophically significant speech—at the cemetery which held the dead of the decisive Battle of Gettysburg. The speaker who came before him, Edward Everett, spoke for more than two hours, while Lincoln's address lasted barely five minutes. Yet in those brief words, composed in the heat of civil war, Lincoln explained the suffering of the day, offered hope for a better future, and recreated the Union. He explained the war and the purpose of the American republic. The war expressed the pangs of a national rebirth, and the nation's purpose was to spread the cause of freedom.

The audience to whom Lincoln spoke could not fully grasp his meaning. Only later, after examining his words in print, did Americans understand. The Gettysburg Address was not a great speech, it was not a truly great piece of literature, but it was an overwhelmingly great philosophical treatise, a summons to national rebirth, fulfillment, and greatness. At the beginning of the year Lincoln had issued a proclamation to emancipate the slaves. Now he issued a proclamation to emancipate the nation.

The Gettysburg Address

Four score and seven years ago our fathers brought forth on this continent, a new nation, conceived in Liberty, and dedicated to the proposition that all men are created equal. Now we are engaged in a great civil war, testing whether that nation, or any nation so conceived and so dedicated, can long endure. We are met on a great battle-field of that war. We have come to dedicate a portion of that field, as a final resting place for those who here gave their lives that that nation might live. It is altogether fitting and proper that we should do this. But, in a larger sense, we can not dedicate—we can not consecrate—we can not hallow—this ground. The brave men, living and dead, who struggled here, have consecrated it, far above our poor power to add or detract. The world will little note, nor long remember what we say here, but it can never forget what they did here. It is for us the living, rather, to be dedicated here to the unfinished work which they who fought here have thus far so nobly advanced. It is rather for us to be here dedicated to the great task remaining before us—that from these honored dead we take increased devotion to that cause for which they gave the last full measure of devotion—that we here highly resolve that these dead shall not have died in vain—that this nation, under God, shall have a new birth of freedom—and that government of the people, by the people, for the people, shall not perish from the earth.

Once more Lincoln's oratory was full of religious language. He placed the nation "under God" and spoke of death and rebirth in a way that identified politics with Christian symbols. He also focused, as had no previous president, on the fact that since the nation was "conceived in Liberty, and dedicated to the proposition that all men are created equal," its purpose, now resurrected, was to extend that freedom. The time of national hypocrisy was over; it was time to finish the task, to fulfill the dream.

THE SECOND INAUGURAL ADDRESS (1865)

On March 4, 1865, Lincoln gave his second inaugural, and last major, address. The Civil War, which had lasted throughout his term in office, was almost won. The Union had been preserved. The slaves had been proclaimed free, and their freedom would be certified with the adoption of the proposed Thirteenth Amendment. In his inaugural speech Lincoln outlined the work left to be done, work that he thought he would live to inspire and lead. He offered a blueprint for peace and reconciliation. Note that the religious language in this speech, which comes in its second half, after his analysis of current and past events, is quite strong.

Fellow Countrymen:

At this second appearing to take the oath of the presidential office, there is less occasion for an extended address than there was at the first. Then a statement, somewhat in detail, of a course to be pursued, seemed fitting and proper. Now, at the expiration of four years, during which public declarations have been constantly called forth on every point and phase of the great contest which still absorbs the attention, and engrosses the energies of the nation, little that is new could be presented. The progress of our arms, upon which all else chiefly depends, is as well known to the public as to myself; and it is, I trust, reasonably satisfactory and encouraging to all. With high hope for the future, no prediction in regard to it is ventured.

On the occasion corresponding to this four years ago, all thoughts were anxiously directed to an impending civil-war. All dreaded it—all sought to avert it. While the inaugural address was being delivered from this place, devoted altogether to *saving* the Union without war, insurgent agents were in the city seeking to destroy it without war—seeking to dissolve the Union, and divide effects, by negotiation. Both parties deprecated war; but one of them would make war rather than let the nation survive; and the other would accept war rather than let it perish. And the war came.

One eighth of the whole population were colored slaves, not distributed generally over the Union, but localized in the southern part of it. These slaves constituted a peculiar and powerful interest. All knew that this interest was, somehow, the cause of the war. To strengthen, perpetuate, and extend this interest was the object for which the insurgents would rend the Union, even by war; while the government claimed no right to do more than to restrict the territorial enlargement of it. Neither party expected for the war, the

(margin note: ⅛ slave population)

magnitude, or the duration, which it has already attained. Neither anticipated that the cause of the conflict might cease with, or even before, the conflict itself should cease. Each looked for an easier triumph, and a result less fundamental and astounding. Both read the same Bible, and pray to the same God; and each invokes His aid against the other. It may seem strange that any men should dare to ask a just God's assistance in wringing their bread from the sweat of other men's faces; but let us judge not that we be not judged.[1] The prayers of both could not be answered; that of neither has been answered fully. The Almighty has His own purposes. "Woe unto the world because of offences! for it must needs be that offences come; but woe to that man by whom the offence cometh!"[2] If we shall suppose that American Slavery is one of those offences which, in the providence of God, must needs come, but which, having continued through His appointed time, He now wills to remove, and that He gives to both North and South, this terrible war, as the woe due to those by whom the offence came, shall we discern therein any departure from those attributes which the believers in a Living God always ascribe to Him? Fondly, do we hope—fervently do we pray—that this mighty scourge of war may speedily pass away. Yet, if God wills that it continue, until all the wealth piled by the bond-man's two hundred and fifty years of unrequited toil shall be sunk, and until every drop of blood drawn with the lash, shall be paid by another drawn with the sword, as was said three thousand years ago, so still it must be said "the judgments of the Lord, are true and righteous altogether."[3]

With malice toward none; with charity for all; with firmness in the right, as God gives us to see the right, let us strive on to finish the work we are in; to build up the nation's wounds; to care for him who shall have borne the battle, and for his widow, and his orphan—to do all which may achieve and cherish a just, and a lasting peace, among ourselves, and with all nations.

Lincoln refers to God twelve times and quotes Scripture three times in twenty-five lines. The latter part of the address is essentially a sermon that uses American religious sentiments to inspire the nation to take on its next task: to build the new nation Lincoln had clearly envisioned in the Gettysburg Address. Lincoln commented to a friend that the speech would not be popular because of the way it reminded people that their way might not be God's

---

[1] Lincoln was paraphrasing Jesus in the Gospel of Matthew 7:1.
[2] Lincoln was quoting Jesus in the Gospel of Matthew 18:7.
[3] Lincoln was quoting Psalm 19:9.

way, but that not to do this would be to deny God's governance of the world.

LINCOLN'S DEATH AND TRANSFIGURATION

Not quite six weeks after his second inauguration, on April 14, Lincoln went to Ford's Theater in Washington to see the play *Our American Cousin.* The South had been beaten, the peace waited to be made. An actor and Southern sympathizer, John Wilkes Booth, entered the president's box and shot Lincoln in the head. He was taken to a house nearby and died the next day without regaining consciousness. Many people noted that it was Easter weekend, that like Jesus he had been killed on Good Friday.

A moment after he was pronounced dead, Secretary of War Edwin Stanton, who had often told people Lincoln was a fool, whispered, "Now he belongs to the ages." This was a prescient comment. Lincoln was about to be transformed in the popular mind, by one of the greatest outpourings of grief in American history, into something no other president had ever been.

Lincoln's funeral procession traveled by train through the loyal states of the Union, stopping in all major cities for memorial services, until at last after twelve days it arrived in Springfield, where the martyred president was buried. Before the journey ended, Lincoln's transformation had already begun. The "fool" was now a hero. The "bumbler" was now the savior of the Union. The "buffoon" was now the man of the people. The man who lacked convictions on slavery was the Great Emancipator. The "agnostic" was now the high priest of the American religion. In time he would become the redeemer of that political-religious system.

Upon Lincoln's death there immediately began a complete reassessment of his character. During the next four years Lincoln was analyzed by countless poets, orators, and biographers, and when William Herndon published his opinion in 1892, readers were eager to learn what the former law partner had to say. While Herndon did not hide Lincoln's faults, as did so many writers in their desire to canonize Lincoln, he did find the Civil War president more than heroic. The essence of Lincoln's character, he said, lay in his power of reason, his conscience, and his sense of right and equity. These were Herndon's conclusions:

> All the follies and wrong Mr. Lincoln ever fell into or committed sprang out of these weak points: the want of intuitive judgment; the lack of quick sagacious knowledge of the play and meaning of men's features as written on the face; the want of the sense of propriety of things; his tenderness and mercy; and lastly, his unsuspecting nature. He was deeply and sincerely honest himself, and assumed that others were so. He never suspected men; and hence in dealing with them he was easily imposed upon.
>
> All the wise and good things Mr. Lincoln ever did sprang out of his great reason, his conscience, his understanding, his heart, his love of the truth, the right, and the good. I am speaking now of his particular and individual faculties and qualities, not of their combination or the result of any combinations. Run out these qualities and faculties abstractly, and see what they produce, a love of the true and the good must, proportioned reasonably and applied practically, produce a man of great power and great humanity.
>
> As illustrative of a combination in Mr. Lincoln's organization, it may be said that his eloquence lay in the strength of his logical faculty, his supreme power of reasoning, his great understanding, and his love of principle; in his clear and accurate vision; in his cool and masterly statement of principles around which the issues gather; and in the statement of those issues and the grouping of the facts that are to carry conviction to the minds of men of every grade of intelligence. He was so clear that he could not be misunderstood or long misrepresented. He stood square and bolt upright to his convictions, and anyone who listened to him would be convinced that he formed his thoughts and utterances by them. His mind was not exactly a wide, broad, generalizing, and comprehensive mind, nor yet a versatile, quick, and subtle one, bounding here and there as emergencies demanded; but it was deep, enduring, strong, like a majestic machine running in deep iron grooves with heavy flanges on its wheels.
>
> Mr. Lincoln himself was a very sensitive man, and hence, in dealing with others, he avoided wounding their hearts or puncturing their sensibility. He was unusually considerate of the feelings of other men, regardless of their rank, condition, or station. At first sight he struck one with his plainness, simplicity of manner, sincerity, candor, and truthfulness. He had no double interests and no overwhelming dignity with which to chill the air around his visitor. He was always easy of approach and thoroughly democratic. He seemed to throw a charm around every man who ever met him. To be in his presence was a pleasure, and no man ever left his company with injured feelings unless most richly deserved.
>
> The universal testimony, "He is an honest man," gave him a firm hold on the masses, and they trusted him with a blind religious

faith. His sad, melancholy face excited their sympathy, and when the dark days came it was their heart-strings that entwined and sustained him. Sympathy, we are told, is one of the strongest and noblest incentives to human action. With the sympathy and love of the people to sustain him, Lincoln had unlimited power over them; he threw an invisible and weightless harness over them, and drove them through disaster and desperation to final victory. The trust and worship by the people of Lincoln were the result of his simple character. He held himself not aloof from the masses. He became one of them. They feared together, they struggled together, they hoped together; thus melted and molded into one, they became one in thought, one in will, one in action. If Lincoln cautiously awaited the full development of the last fact in the great drama before he acted, when longer waiting would be a crime, he knew that the people were determinedly at his back. Thus, when a blow was struck, it came with the unerring aim and power of a bolt from heaven. A natural king—not ruling men, but leading them along the drifts and trends of their own tendencies, always keeping in mind the consent of the governed, he developed what the future historian will call the sublimest order of conservative statesmanship.

Whatever of life, vigor, force, and power of eloquence his peculiar qualities gave him; whatever there was in a fair, manly, honest, and impartial administration of justice under law to all men at all times; whatever there was in a strong will in the right governed by tenderness and mercy; whatever there was in toil and sublime patience; whatever there was in these things or a wise combination of them, Lincoln is justly entitled to in making up the impartial verdict of history. These limit and define him as a statesman, as an orator, as an executive of the nation, and as a man. They developed in all the walks of his life; they were his law; they were his nature, they were Abraham Lincoln.

This long, bony, sad man floated down the Sangamon river [4] in a frail canoe in the spring of 1831. Like a piece of driftwood he lodged at last, without a history, strange, penniless, and alone. In sight of the capital of Illinois, in the fatigue of daily toil he struggled for the necessaries of life. Thirty years later this same peculiar man left the Sangamon river, backed by friends, by power, by the patriotic prayers of millions of people, to be the ruler of the greatest nation in the world.

As the leader of a brave people in their desperate struggle for national existence, Abraham Lincoln will always be an interesting historical character. His strong, honest, sagacious, and noble life will always possess a peculiar charm. Had it not been for his conservative statesmanship, his supreme confidence in the wisdom of the people, his extreme care in groping his way among facts and before ideas,

---

[4] The Sangamon flows into the Illinois, which flows into the Mississippi.

this nation might have been two governments today. The low and feeble circulation of his blood; his healthful irritability, which responded so slowly to the effects of stimuli; the strength of his herculean frame; his peculiar organism, conserving its force; his sublime patience; his wonderful endurance; his great hand and heart, saved this country from division, when division meant its irreparable ruin.

The central figure of our national history, the sublime type of our civilization, posterity, with the record of his career and actions before it, will decree that, whether Providence so ordained it or not, Abraham Lincoln was the man for the hour.

Long before Herndon penned these words Lincoln had grown, in the American public's estimation, to Herculean stature and influence. Herndon only gave concrete expression to an impression that had been made indelibly on the American mind: Abraham Lincoln was immortal.

A QUEST FOR IMMORTALITY: THE ANDERSON THESIS

The life Lincoln lived, particularly his words and deeds as president, established his titanic image and his immortal influence. In life he changed America; after death he played a role in national affairs that was fully as powerful as his role in life.

Historians have long speculated on Lincoln's awareness of his role—in life and in death—and to what extent he sought it, molded it to suit his goals, and courted the immortality he achieved. Those who believe dreams can reveal significant clues to a person's inner fears and hopes like to recall a dream Lincoln admitted having just nights before he was killed. It frightened him, and he kept it secret for a time; but then one night, sitting with Mrs. Lincoln and a few friends, when the conversation turned to dreams, he admitted that he was haunted by one. Carl Sandburg recounts the conversation as recorded later by Lincoln's friend Ward Hill Lamon.

Mrs. Lincoln remarked, "Why, you look dreadfully solemn, do *you* believe in dreams?" "I can't say that I do," returned Mr. Lincoln; "but I had one the other night which has haunted me ever since. After it occurred, the first time I opened the Bible, strange as it may appear, it was at the twenty-eighth chapter of Genesis, which relates the wonderful dream Jacob had. I turned to other passages, and seemed

to encounter a dream or a vision wherever I looked. I kept on turning the leaves of the old book, and everywhere my eye fell upon passages recording matters strangely in keeping with my own thoughts,—supernatural visitations, dreams, visions, etc."
He now looked so serious and disturbed that Mrs. Lincoln exclaimed: "You frighten me! What is the matter?" "I am afraid," said Mr. Lincoln, seeing the effect his words had upon his wife, "that I have done wrong to mention the subject at all; but somehow the thing has got possession of me, and, like Banquo's ghost,[5] it will not down."
This set on fire Mrs. Lincoln's curiosity. Though saying she didn't believe in dreams, she kept at him to tell what it was he had seen in his sleep that now had such a hold on him. He hesitated, waited a little, slowly began, his face in shadows of melancholy:
"About ten days ago I retired very late. I had been up waiting for important dispatches from the front. I could not have been long in bed when I fell into a slumber, for I was weary. I soon began to dream. There seemed to be a death-like stillness about me. Then I heard subdued sobs, as if a number of people were weeping. I thought I left my bed and wandered downstairs. There the silence was broken by the same pitiful sobbing, but the mourners were invisible. I went from room to room; no living person was in sight, but the same mournful sounds of distress met me as I passed along. It was light in all the rooms; every object was familiar to me; but where were all the people who were grieving as if their hearts would break? I was puzzled and alarmed. What could be the meaning of all this? Determined to find the cause of a state of things so mysterious and so shocking, I kept on until I arrived at the East Room, which I entered. There I met with a sickening surprise. Before me was a catafalque, on which rested a corpse wrapped in funeral vestments. Around it were stationed soldiers who were acting as guards; and there was a throng of people, some gazing mournfully upon the corpse, whose face was covered, others weeping pitifully. 'Who is dead in the White House?' I demanded of one of the soldiers. 'The President,' was his answer; 'he was killed by an assassin!' Then came a loud burst of grief from the crowd, which awoke me from my dream. I slept no more that night; and although it was only a dream, I have been strangely annoyed by it ever since."
"That is horrid!" said Mrs. Lincoln. "I wish you had not told it. I am glad I don't believe in dreams, or I should be in terror from this time forth." "Well," responded Mr. Lincoln, thoughtfully, "it is only a dream, Mary. Let us say no more about it, and try to forget it."
The dream had shaken its dreamer to the depths, noted Lamon. As he had give the secret of it to others he was "grave,

---

[5] In Shakespeare's play, Banquo was a friend of Macbeth. Banquo's ghost returns to accuse Macbeth of killing the true king.

gloomy, and at times visibly pale, but perfectly calm." To Lamon afterward, in a reference to it Lincoln quoted from *Hamlet*, "To sleep; perchance to dream! ay, *there's the rub!*"—stressing the last three words.

The historian Dwight G. Anderson has studied this dream in the context of Lincoln's career and political philosophy. He is convinced that it reflected Lincoln's ambivalent feelings about George Washington, the first and most admired president, the one he claimed to revere as a father figure but had during his tenure in the White House betrayed and in a political sense "murdered."

Lincoln's observers have always assumed that this dream foreshadowed his own death by assassination. The dream, however, did not reveal the identity of the dead president. . . . Lincoln said the face of the corpse was covered. Moreover, Lincoln himself seemed specifically to rule out the possibility that he was the dead president by later telling Lamon, who was distressed by Lincoln's disregard for his own safety, "For a long time you have been trying to keep somebody—the Lord knows who—from killing me. Don't you see how it will turn out? In this dream it was not me, but some other fellow, that was killed. It seems that this ghostly assassin tried his hand on someone else."

If not Lincoln, who was the dead president? The only other possibility suggested by the contextual evidence is that the president of Lincoln's dream was George Washington and Lincoln his "ghostly assassin." That this possibility is also suggested by an examination of Lincoln's personal psychology and political history lends credence to this assumption. For George Washington, it can be shown, provided Lincoln with an imaginary father whom he both emulated and defied, and finally, by ceremonial apotheosis, elevated to divine rank. If the guilt that Lincoln experienced in achieving this symbolic victory over Washington haunted him like Banquo's ghost, it also provided the psychological basis for Lincoln's refoundation of political authority in the United States.

Lincoln's personal psychology became bound up with the history of the nation through the influence of Mason Locke Weems's *Life of Washington*. This book, which Lincoln read repeatedly as a youth, offered him two contradictory models of political success. One was that of Washington himself, who according to Weems achieved his great stature because of his private virtues. The other was that of a "cunning, ambitious, unprincipled" man who would seek greatness on "the ruins of public liberty"—the figure against whom Washington warned the nation in his Farewell Address. Lincoln followed both models sequentially. At first he sought political success by upholding Washington's advice and example; failing there, he seized upon the alternative, eventually presiding over the destruction of Washington's Union, and becoming the very tyrant against whom Washington had warned. Sublimating guilt into political authority, Lincoln took Washington's place as the father of his country. . . .

Lincoln was always careful to emulate the style of Washington, especially his modesty and humility. During his early years, he apparently modeled himself on the father of his country. On his way to Washington, D.C., to assume the presidency, he used the first president as the standard by which to assess the task before him. Once in office, he invoked Washington's legacy as a source of authority. Yet after proclaiming Washington's birthday as a national day of celebration in 1862, to be marked by public readings of the Farewell Address, Lincoln made virtually no further reference to Washington. It was as if Washington had suddenly ceased to exist. And in a way he had: the proclamation of his birthday as a national holiday signified his apotheosis, and thus his removal from the seat of authority—a place thereafter to be occupied by Lincoln himself.

There are several intriguing aspects to Lincoln's statement that his dream of the dead president haunted him like Banquo's ghost. First is the identification suggested by Lincoln between himself and Macbeth.[6] He had long been an admirer of this Shakespearean tragedy; telegraph operators often noticed him carrying a worn copy of the play, and he had written in 1863, "I think nothing equals Macbeth." Following his triumphant visit to Richmond in April 1865, he had read aloud from the play, dwelling at length on a particular passage: "The lines after the murder of Duncan, when the new king falls a prey to moral torment, were dramatically dwelt on. Now and then he paused to expatiate on how exact a picture Shakespeare here gives of a murderer's mind when, the dark deed achieved, its perpetrator already envies his victim's calm sleep." Lincoln's observers, by naively assuming that he was making a comparison here between the Confederacy and Macbeth, have overlooked the more plausible parallel between Lincoln and Macbeth: both were fascinating characters, capable of great goodness but driven by ambition to defy the gods; men entrapped by "necessity" in a process of violence, but who had the intelligence to foresee the consequences of their acts, and the sensitivity to accept the burdens of guilt that lesser men might have ignored.

The obvious similarity between Duncan and George Washington strengthens the assumption that Lincoln saw himself as Mac-

---

[6] Anderson also notes the connection in Lincoln's mind between the two Shakespearean tragedies *Hamlet* and *Macbeth*. Both address the dastardly deed of killing one's lord.

beth. When Macbeth is contemplating the assassination of Duncan, he considers the reasons for not going through with it. He is, after all, both Duncan's kinsman and subject. "Besides," Macbeth says, "this Duncan / Hath borne his faculties so meek, hath been / So clear in his great office, that his virtues / Will plead like angels . . . And pity . . . Shall blow the horrid deed in every eye, / That tears shall drown the wind." By comparison, Macbeth has only his "vaulting ambition" to sustain him. There was, in addition, the inescapable implication of guilt in Lincoln's statement that his dream haunted him like Banquo's ghost: the ghost is but a projection of Macbeth's guilt. More important, in terms of understanding Lincoln's anxieties, Banquo's ghost is also a reminder of the witches' prophecy that it is Banquo's paternal authority, rather than Macbeth's, that is to be perpetuated. But if Lincoln, like Macbeth, feared that the monuments created by his bloody hand would not last, his anxieties must have been calmed somewhat by the other literary reference he recalled as he told about the dream of the dead president: the biblical story of Jacob's dream.

In telling about his dream, Lincoln said, "After it occurred, the first time I opened the Bible, strange as it may appear, it was at the twenty-eighth chapter of Genesis, which relates the wonderful dream Jacob had." The wonder of Jacob's dream was that the God of Abraham and Isaac appeared to him in it and promised that Jacob's paternal line would be extended and blessed, even though he was not the legitimate heir. Born holding onto Esau's heel, Jacob had forced Esau to relinquish his birthright as the firstborn son, and succeeded in deceiving their father, Isaac, so that the father's blessing, rightfully Esau's, was given to Jacob instead. Jacob's dream held out the promise of immortality to Jacob and his descendants, though Jacob lived in fear that Esau would someday seek his revenge.

A thematic link between Banquo's ghost and Jacob's dream is provided not simply by guilt over acts of usurpation, but also by anxiety about legitimacy and fear that symbols of immortality might be destroyed. It was a theme that Lincoln well understood. If he could view himself as Macbeth, tortured by guilt for his crimes, he could also recall himself as Banquo, the loyal and virtuous subject. If he could conceive of himself as Jacob, the unscrupulous pretender, he could also imagine himself as Esau, the firstborn and legitimate heir. In other words, if he could see himself as the cunning tyrant against whom Washington had warned, he could also recollect his identity as Weems's Washington, upholder of virtue and constitutional order. The fool had entered fields where angels feared to tread; but, in the end, the "better angels" of his nature seemed to prevail.

It was with "malice toward none and charity for all" that Lincoln wanted to bring the war to an end. He proposed to end it, as he said in 1864, by the "Christian principle of forgiveness on terms of repentance." His Second Inaugural Address, which combined pity for all with compassion for the guilty, transformed his own guilt into a doctrine by which all might be forgiven. Whether or not Lincoln intended to cast himself in the role of Christ, his contemporaries were more than willing to draw the parallels. By his death, Lincoln became the savior of the republic, one who, by his sacrifice and atonement, redeemed the sins of the fathers and gave to the nation a new life, a life everlasting.

Summary: Wit and Conviction

Without the wit he learned in his rise from poverty to prominence, Lincoln could never have survived the demands of the presidency, particularly its requirements at that moment of history. With his wit he was able temporarily to lift his terrible burdens and teach the nation lessons it could not have learned from heavy treatises.

Without the convictions he developed during and following his mid-life crisis, he could never have saved and transformed the United States from a nation crippled by hypocrisy to one able to reach for the heights of its better nature. His convictions refocused a simple call to preserve the Union to a challenge to emancipate its people, black and white, from the tyranny of slavery.

The Lincoln wit and the Lincoln convictions made possible his victory over death. They transform a tawdry killing into a sacrificial martyrdom. They made a mortal immortal.

Questions for Responsive Essays

1. How did Lincoln use his First Inaugural Address to communicate his goals as president to the public? What are these goals, and how does Lincoln rationally detail them? How does he see his own duty as president?

2. How did Lincoln use humor to teach lessons? What were the sources of his wit? How might it have helped him carry his heavy burden?

3. Why is the Gettysburg Address considered poor oratory but great philosophy? In what ways did it refocus the purposes of the war and the nation? How does it use religious language to make its points?

4. In what ways does Lincoln's Second Inaugural Address differ from his First? What are his concerns in it—both old and new? How does it once again use religious language to buttress his message?

5. Analyze Anderson's theory about Lincoln's "quest for immortality." What are its strengths and weaknesses? Did Lincoln think he was Washington's assassin? How else might his dream be explained? Did Lincoln indeed betray Washington's legacy?

PART III

Lincoln the Liberator

Lincoln entered the White House convinced that while he hated slavery and opposed its extension into the western territories, he could not under the Constitution end it where it legally existed. He said so in no uncertain terms in his debates with Douglas and in his First Inaugural Address.

An early visitor to the Lincoln White House bluntly pointed out to Lincoln the irony that a poorly educated prairie politician should be president at the moment of the nation's greatest crisis. Lincoln readily agreed with him and admitted that he had no grand solution to the crisis and was merely acting one day at a time. His plan was simply to try to preserve the Union, and he feared that freeing the slaves, even if he could do so constitutionally, would further alienate the slave states he wished to keep within or reattract to that Union.

Then, in 1862, needing to energize and refocus the faltering war effort in response to pressure from the more radical members of his wavering coalition, he began to change his mind. On January 1, 1863, he issued the Emancipation Proclamation. This proclamation did not end slavery, and Lincoln soon began to make plans for the constitutional amendment that would do so in 1865. But this statement of purpose, which acted as a sort of shock therapy to galvanize Union forces and allowed Lincoln to assume the high moral ground, was perhaps his most significant deed as president and earned Lincoln the epithet "the Great Liberator."

YOUNG LINCOLN ON SLAVERY

During his eight years in the Illinois legislature, the young Lincoln gave few signs that he would one day be the man who freed the slaves. He spent most of his time there working for new roads, investigating government fraud, and supporting the drive for a new capitol, all important but rather mundane political activities. Once he and a colleague did offer a resolution that took issue with the legislative majority's statement on slavery, but this statement was typically moderate, or Whiggish. It was offered on March 3, 1837, when Lincoln was twenty-eight years of age.

> Resolutions upon the subject of domestic slavery having passed both branches of the General Assembly at its present session, the undersigned hereby protest against the passage of the same.
>
> They believe that the institution of slavery is founded on both injustice and bad policy; but that the promulgation of abolition doctrines tends rather to increase than to abate its evils.
>
> They believe that the Congress of the United States has no power, under the constitution, to interfere with the institution of slavery in the different States.
>
> They believe that the Congress of the United States has the power, under the constitution, to abolish slavery in the District of Columbia; but that that power ought not to be exercised unless at the request of the people of said District.
>
> The difference between these opinions and those contained in the said resolutions, is their reason for entering this protest.
>
> Dan Stone,
> A. Lincoln,
> Representatives from the county of Sangamon.

Nor is Lincoln the Liberator to be found in the following letter, dated September 27, 1841, when Lincoln was thirty-two, in which he makes some informal observations about slavery. Written to Mary Speed, whose home he had visited in Louisville, it describes his steamboat trip back to Springfield with Mary's brother Joshua. His major impression of the slaves on board the craft was of their contentment. He may not have approved of slavery, but at this point he seems not to have had a passionate desire to end it.

> We got on board the Steam Boat Lebanon in the locks of the Canal about 12. o'clock. M. of the day we left, and reached St. Louis the next Monday at 8 P.M. Nothing of interest happened during the passage, except the vexatious delays occasioned by the sand bars we

thought interesting. By the way, a fine example was presented on board the boat for contemplating the effect of *condition* upon human happiness. A gentleman had purchased twelve negroes in different parts of Kentucky and was taking them to a farm in the South. They were chained six and six together. A small iron clevis was around the left wrist of each, and this fastened to the main chain by a shorter one at a convenient distance from the others; so that the negroes were strung together precisely like so many fish upon a trot-line. In this condition they were being separated forever from the scenes of their childhood, their friends, their fathers and mothers, and brothers and sisters, and many of them, from their wives and children, and going in to perpetual slavery where the lash of the master is proverbially more ruthless and unrelenting than any other where; and yet amid all these distressing circumstances, as we would think them, they were the most cheerful and apparently happy creatures on board. One, whose offence for which he had been sold was an over-fondness for his wife, played the fiddle almost continually; and the others danced, sung, cracked jokes, and played various games with cards from day to day. How true it is that "God tempers the wind to the shorn lamb," or in other words, that He renders the worst of human conditions tolerable, while he permits the best, to be nothing better than tolerable.

THE ROAD TO EMANCIPATION: A RE-CREATION BY STEPHEN B. OATES

Nothing in Lincoln's early life, nothing in his one term in Congress, nothing even in his race for president or his first year and a half in the White House presaged his role as the Great Emancipator. The prominent Lincoln biographer Stephen B. Oates, in his book *With Malice Toward None: The Life of Abraham Lincoln,* describes the disappointment of many abolitionists when, by July 4, 1861, Lincoln had taken no action, after four months in the White House, to free the slaves.

On July 4, Congress assembled with talk of an impending battle echoing across the capital—and Lincoln sent over an Independence Day message in which he set forth the central issue in this contest. And that was whether a constitutional republic, a democracy, could preserve itself. There were those in Europe who argued that rebellion and anarchy were inherent weaknesses of a republic and that an enlightened monarchy was the more stable form of government. "Must a government, of necessity, be too strong for the liberties of its own people, or too weak to maintain its own existence?" Lincoln asked. No, he believed that America's popular government could survive the present crisis. But to do so the government must meet force with force. It must teach dissidents "the folly of being the beginners of a war." It must show the world "that those who can fairly carry an election, can also suppress a rebellion," and that a constitutional republic was a workable system which offered hope for people everywhere, as he'd long contended. "This is essentially a People's contest," he declared. "On the side of the Union, it is a struggle for maintaining in the world, that form, and substance of government, whose leading object is, to elevate the condition of men—to lift artificial weights from all shoulders—to clear the paths of laudable pursuit for all—to afford all, an unfettered start, and a fair chance, in the race of life."

These were noble words indeed, but what about black people? What about the slaves? Did they not deserve "an unfettered start, and a fair chance, in the race of life," just like white people? How could Lincoln deliver these eloquent phrases and yet insist that the termination of human bondage in a "free" America was not a war objective? So went the arguments of abolitionist leaders such as William Garrison and Frederick Douglass, who exhorted Lincoln to issue an emancipation decree.

Nor were abolitionists the only people who objected to Lincoln's policy on slavery. Liberal Republicans Charles Sumner, Benjamin Wade, and Zachariah Chandler also objected. Before and after Lincoln's congressional message, they secluded themselves with Lincoln in his White House office, and Sumner even accompanied the president on his carriage rides. Chandler, a senator from Michigan, was a Detroit businessman who had amassed a fortune in real estate and dry goods. A restless, rawboned New Englander who had migrated west to make money and history, he was smooth-shaven and wore an eternally grim expression, his mouth turned down at the corners. Bluff Ben Wade, a senator from Ohio, was short and thick-chested, with iron-gray hair, sunken black eyes, and a square beardless face. A pugnacious individual known for "a certain bulldog obduracy" and a readiness to duel with Southerners, Wade had little patience with what he saw as an indecisive, slow-moving president. He hated slavery, as Sumner and Chandler did. But Wade was also prejudiced against Negroes; he complained about their odor, and growled about the Negro cooks who had served him in Washington, remarking that he had eaten so much food "cooked by Niggers until I can smell and taste the Nigger all over." Like many other Republicans, he thought the best solution to America's race problem was to ship all black people back to Africa.

Now, in their conferences with Lincoln, the three senators wanted to make the annihilation of slavery a Union war objective. Before secession, of course, they had emphatically endorsed the party's hands-off policy regarding slavery in the South. But civil war had removed their constitutional scruples about the issue. Now they argued that either the president or Congress could remove the peculiar institution by the war powers, and they wanted Lincoln to do it. If he emancipated the slaves, he would maim and cripple the Confederacy and hasten an end to the rebellion. Sumner flatly asserted that slavery and the rebellion were "wedded" and would stand or fall together.

Lincoln was sympathetic to their argument. Personally he detested human bondage as much as they did. He was also anxious to maintain a close working relationship with Republican liberals, who, though a minority, still controlled most of the powerful congressional committees. Moreover, he had great respect for the liberals, thought them completely dedicated Republicans, and referred to men like Sumner as the conscience of the party.

Yet Lincoln would not free the slaves. As president, he was responsible to the entire country, which obliged him to move with extreme caution and care, and in 1861 most of the country seemed to him steadfastly opposed to emancipation even as a war measure. If he violated his pledge to leave slavery alone as an institution by issuing an emancipation proclamation, the consequences, he feared, would be calamitous. Emancipation would almost surely drive the loyal border states out of the Union, alienate Northern Democrats, destroy the bipartisan war coalition that had begun to form after Fort Sumter, and might even ignite a racial powder keg in the North. Then the Union really would be lost. Thus Lincoln stuck to his policy of fighting the war strictly to save the Union. He would crush the rebellion with the army and restore national authority in the South with slavery still intact. At the same time, Lincoln and his party would implement their policy of slave containment, sealing it up in the Southern states, and putting it on the road to ultimate doom.

Two months later, in September 1861, Lincoln angrily revoked a proclamation of emancipation issued for the southern section of Missouri by Commander John C. Frémont.[1] Abolitionists, including Frémont, began to believe that in Lincoln the nation had elected a Southern sympathizer.

Through 1861 and much of 1862 Lincoln continued to act cautiously, perhaps because he still doubted his constitutional powers, perhaps because he still hoped to bring the secessionist states back into the fold, perhaps because he did not know what the United States would do with freed slaves. A man of his times,

---

[1] Frémont, who had "liberated" California from Spain in 1846 and served as its first president before it joined the Union, had been the Republican Party's first presidential nominee in 1856.

he personally doubted that blacks and whites could ever live together in harmony as equals.

AN ADDRESS TO FREE BLACKS

We find evidence of Lincoln's doubts about racial equality in a speech he made to a delegation of Northern free blacks, then called "colored," who visited him at the White House on August 14, 1862. Some of his assumptions and proposals may surprise readers who think Lincoln envisioned a post-war society of racial equality and harmony.

Perhaps you have long been free, or all your lives. Your race are suffering, in my judgment, the greatest wrong inflicted on any people. but even when you cease to be slaves, you are yet far removed from being placed on an equality with the white race. You are cut off from many of the advantages which the other race enjoy. The aspiration of men is to enjoy equality with the best when free, but on this broad continent, not a single man of your race is made the equal of a single man of ours. Go where you are treated the best, and the ban is still upon you.

I do not propose to discuss this, but to present it as a fact with which we have to deal. I cannot alter it if I would. It is a fact, about which we all think and feel alike, I and you. We look to our condition, owing to the existence of the two races on this continent. I need not recount to you the effects upon white men, growing out of the institution of Slavery. I believe in its general evil effects on the white race. See our present condition—the country engaged in war!—our white men cutting one another's throats, none knowing how far it will extend; and then consider what we know to be the truth. But for your race among us there could not be war, although many men engaged on either side do not care for you one way or the other. Nevertheless, I repeat, without the institution of Slavery and the colored race as a basis, the war could not have an existence.

It is better for us both, therefore, to be separated. I know that there are free men among you, who even if they could better their condition are not as much inclined to go out of the country as those, who being slaves could obtain their freedom on this condition. I suppose one of the principal difficulties in the way of colonization is that the free colored man cannot see that his comfort would be advanced by it. You may believe you can live in Washington or elsewhere in the United States the remainder of your life, perhaps more so than you can in any foreign country, and hence you may come to the conclusion that you have nothing to do with the idea of going to a foreign country. This is (I speak in no unkind sense) an extremely selfish view of the case.

The place I am thinking about having for a colony is in Central America. It is nearer to us than Liberia [where American slaves had gone in years past]—not much more than one-fourth as far as Liberia, and within seven days' run by steamers. Unlike Liberia it is on a great line of travel—it is a highway. The country is a very excellent one for any people, and with great natural resources and advantages, and especially because of the similarity of climate with your native land—thus being suited to your physical condition.

The particular place I have in view is to be a great highway from the Atlantic or Caribbean Sea to the Pacific Ocean, and this particular place has all the advantages for a colony.[2] On both sides there are harbors among the finest in the world. Again, there is evidence of very rich coal mines. A certain amount of coal is valuable in any country, and there may be more than enough for the wants of the country. Why I attach so much importance to coal is, it will afford an opportunity to the inhabitants for immediate employment till they get ready to settle permanently in their homes.

I shall, if I get a sufficient number of you engaged, have provisions made that you shall not be wronged. If you will engage in the enterprise I will spend some of the money intrusted to me. I am not sure you will succeed. The Government may lose the money, but we cannot succeed unless we try; but we think, with care, we can succeed.

The practical thing I want to ascertain is whether I can get a number of able-bodied men, with their wives and children, who are willing to go, when I present evidence of encouragement and protection. Could I get a hundred tolerably intelligent men, with their wives and children, to "cut their own fodder," so to speak? Can I have fifty? If I could find twenty-five able-bodied men, with a mixture of women and children, good things in the family relation, I think I could make a successful commencement.

I want you to let me know whether this can be done or not. This is the practical part of my wish to see you. These are subjects of very great importance, worthy of a month's study, instead of a speech delivered in an hour. I ask you then to consider seriously not pertaining to yourselves merely, nor for your race, and ours, for the present time, but as one of the things, if successfully managed, for the good of mankind—not confined to the present generation, but as
"From age to age descends the lay
To millions yet to be,
Till far its echoes roll away,
Into eternity."

---

[2] Lincoln was referring to a plan by the Chiriqui Improvement Company to resettle freedmen in various Central American countries.

NEARING EMANCIPATION: OATES CONTINUES

Lincoln's address to the black delegation in August 1862 showed he was looking ahead to a time when slaves would be free, but that he felt they could not live in peace in the United States and had no immediate plan to free them. Only a month later, however, with the war stretching on without apparent end and the last hope of compromise with secessionists gone, he decided to take executive action and issue a proclamation of emancipation. Between September 22 and 24 he wrote a preliminary draft. Oates once more tells the story.

> What troubled Lincoln now was what to do with the liberated slaves. By now the Chiriqui colonization project[3] had fizzled out, mainly because several Latin American countries objected to a U.S. colony in their midst and threatened to keep it out by force. So Lincoln crossed off Chiriqui, with growing doubts as to whether colonization was a workable solution to the race question anyway. If by some miracle the Union did win this war and four million Southern Negroes were ultimately freed, the cost of transporting all black people out of America would be astronomical, not to mention expenses for housing, shelter, and food to get them started in some new land. And in any case most Northern blacks seemed intractably opposed to colonization, which meant that it couldn't be brought off voluntarily as Lincoln insisted it must. Still, he wanted to leave all possibilities open—and above all to pacify Northern whites. So late in December he signed a contract with white promoters to resettle five thousand Negro volunteers on Haiti's Isle of Vache. Thus when Lincoln's proclamation took effect, he could show Northern whites that a colonization project was still on the drawing boards.
>
> Nevertheless, Lincoln had just about decided that the fate of former slaves would have to be worked out in the South itself, that the white and black races in America would have to learn how to live with one another. He had a general idea that Southern "colored people" could be utilized as a free work force and be hired out to their former masters at decent wages, thus preventing the blacks from coming North as white people feared. He'd made an oblique reference to this in his recent message to Congress and would do so again in his final proclamation. But how to implement his idea? How to merge

---

[3] The project Lincoln referred to in his address to the Northern black Americans had failed mainly because Central American countries feared the United States would use the pretense of protecting freed blacks to annex host nations.

whites and free blacks without causing racial friction in South and North alike? He had no answer to that.

But he had reached a decision about able-bodied black men—something Sumner, Stanton, and others had urged on him for some time now. He would enlist blacks in the army—Southern slaves and Northern free Negroes—and would say so in his final proclamation. If he'd opposed this earlier in the rebellion, mainly out of concern for the border states, the terrible exigencies of the war had impelled him to change his mind. The fact was that the Union desperately needed black manpower, what with recruiting falling off sharply this winter and Union armies suffering troop shortages on all fronts. "The colored population," Lincoln said, "is the great available and yet unavailed of, force for restoring the Union," and he meant to avail himself of that force and to use the blacks as soldiers, not as menials. And though he was not quite ready to throw them into the front lines as combat troops, he would employ them extensively as garrison soldiers, thus liberating thousands of whites from garrison duty so that they could fight. . . .

That night [December 31–January 1] Lincoln tossed in fitful sleep, dreaming of corpses on a distant battlefield in Tennessee, of guns flashing in the night, of silent troops lying exhausted in the rain, of crowds reading casualty returns at Willard's Hotel. He woke in the darkness and lay there until the first gray of morning spread through his chamber. Tired and trembling from the night, he made his way down to the shop and lit the fireplace and gas lamps. So it was the dawn of a new year and the rebellion continued with no foreseeable end. What had begun as a ninety-day skirmish to restore the old Union had now swelled into a cataclysmic upheaval, forcing Lincoln to hurl an edict like a lance at the heart of the rebel South. As Lincoln told an Indiana senator, the war was the supreme irony of his life: that he who sickened at the sight of blood, who abhorred stridency and physical violence, should be cast in the middle of a great civil war, a tornado of blood and wreckage with consequences beyond prediction for those swept up in its winds.

At his desk, he put the final touches on his proclamation and then read it to make sure the words were right.

As of this day, the document said, all slaves in the rebellious states were "forever free." "For the present," the following areas were exempted from emancipation: those Louisiana parishes behind Union lines, certain occupied places in Virginia, the counties of West Virginia (which had recently separated from the rebels and would soon be admitted into the Union as a new state), the state of Tennessee, now under the military governorship of Andrew Johnson, and the entire loyal border. In issuing this decree, the President admonished the slaves to refrain from "unnecessary violence" and remain in the South working for "reasonable wages." Those slaves and free Negroes who so desired might now enlist in the Union army, "to garrison forts, positions, stations, and other places," and might sail on Union warships. "And upon this act," the President concluded, "sincerely believed to be an act of justice, warranted by the Constitution, upon military necessity, I invoke the considerate judgment of mankind, and the gracious favor of Almighty God." . . .

In the afternoon, Lincoln returned to his office for the signing of the emancipation proclamation. It was a casual affair, as Seward and several other Cabinet members and public officials wandered in. At the table, Lincoln dipped a gold pen in ink, but his hand trembled badly and he put the pen down. He assured everyone that he was never more certain of doing right. "If my name ever goes into history," he said, "it will be for this act." But he'd been shaking hands for hours and his right arm was "almost paralyzed." He worried that a nervous signature would invite his critics to say, "he hesitated." "But anyway it is going to be done." Then he took the pen and slowly and carefully wrote out his full name. There, he said, "that will do."

Out the proclamation went to an anxious nation. The reactions would come sweeping back soon enough, and Lincoln braced himself for the worst. Beyond the White House, a black preacher named Henry M. Turner ran down Pennsylvania Avenue with a copy of the proclamation and tried to read it to an assembly of Negroes. Out of breath, he gave the proclamation to a Mr. Hinton, who read it "with great force and earnestness," and the blacks broke into uninhibited demonstrations, shouted, clapped, and sang of jubilee while dogs barked at their sides. Presently an interracial crowd gathered in front of the White House and called for the President. When he appeared at the window and bowed to them, the blacks cheered Lincoln,—cried out in ecstasy, and said if he would come out of that palace, they would hug him to death. "Preacher Turner exclaimed that 'it was indeed a time of times,' that 'nothing like it will ever be seen again in this life.'"

THE EMANCIPATION PROCLAMATION

The following is the official proclamation, issued January 1, 1863. It is based on the preliminary one of September but incorporates a few improvements. Contemporeaneous commentators on the subject of the presidential proclamation would refer to the preliminary form until this official proclamation was issued.

BY THE PRESIDENT OF THE UNITED STATES OF AMERICA
A PROCLAMATION.

Whereas, on the twentysecond day of September, in the year of our Lord one thousand eight hundred and sixty two, a proclamation was

...ward to them that, in all cases when allowed, they labor faithfully for reasonable wages.

And I further declare and make known, that such persons of suitable condition, will be received into the armed service of the United States to garrison forts, positions, stations, and other places, and to man vessels of all sorts in said service.

And upon this act, sincerely believed to be an act of justice, warranted by the Constitution, upon military necessity, I invoke the considerate judgment of mankind, and the gracious favor of Almighty God.

In witness whereof, I have hereunto set my hand and caused the seal of the United States to be affixed.

Done at the city of Washington, this first day of January, in the year of our Lord one thousand eight hundred and sixty three, and of the Independence of the United States of America the eighty-seventh.

Abraham Lincoln

By the President:

William H. Seward,
Secretary of State.

With the words of the Emancipation Proclamation, President Lincoln on January 1, 1863, took the first bold step toward freeing the American slaves.

issued by the President of the United States, containing, among other things, the following, towit:

"That on the first day of January, in the year of our Lord one thousand eight hundred and sixty-three, all persons held as slaves within any State or designated part of a State, the people whereof shall then be in rebellion against the United States, shall be then, thenceforward, and forever free; and the Executive Government of the United States, including the military and naval authority thereof, will recognize and maintain the freedom of such persons, and will do no act or acts to repress such persons, or any of them, in any efforts they may make for their actual freedom.

"That the Executive will, on the first day of January aforesaid, by proclamation, designate the States and parts of States, if any, in which the people thereof, respectively, shall then be in rebellion against the United States; and the fact that any State, or the people thereof, shall on that day be, in good faith, represented in the Congress of the United States by members chosen thereto at elections wherein a majority of the qualified voters of such State shall have participated, shall, in the absence of strong countervailing testimony, be deemed conclusive evidence that such State, and the people thereof, are not then in rebellion against the United States."

Now, therefore I, Abraham Lincoln, President of the United States, by virtue of the power in me vested as Commander-in-Chief of the Army and Navy of the United States in time of actual armed rebellion against authority and government of the United States, and as a fit and necessary war measure for suppressing said rebellion, do, on this first day of January, in the year of our lord one thousand eight hundred and sixty three, and in accordance with my purpose so to do publicly proclaimed for the full period of one hundred days, from the day first above mentioned, order and designate as the States and parts of States wherein the people thereof respectively, are this day in rebellion against the United States, the following, towit:

Arkansas, Texas, Louisiana, (except the Parishes of St. Bernard, Plaquemines, Jefferson, St. Johns, St. Charles, St. James, Ascension, Assumption, Terrebonne, Lafourche, St. Mary, St. Martin, and Orleans, including the City of New-Orleans) Mississippi, Alabama, Florida, Georgia, South-Carolina, North Carolina, and Virginia, (except the forty eight counties designated as West Virginia, and also the counties of Berkley, Accomac, Northampton, Elizabeth-City, York, Princess Ann, and Norfolk, including the cities of Norfolk & Portsmouth); and which excepted parts are, for the present, left precisely as if this proclamation were not issued.

And by virtue of the power, and for the purpose aforesaid, I do order and declare that all persons held as slaves within said designated States, and parts of States, are, and henceforward shall be free; and that the Executive government of the United States, including the military and naval authorities thereof, will recognize and maintain the freedom of said persons.

And I hereby enjoin upon the people so declared to be free to abstain from all violence, unless in necessary self-defence; and I recommend to them that, in all cases when allowed, they labor faithfully for reasonable wages.

And I further declare and make known, that such persons of suitable condition, will be received into the armed service of the United States to garrison forts, positions, stations, and other places, and to man vessels of all sorts in said service.

And upon this act, sincerely believed to be an act of justice, warranted by the Constitution, upon military necessity, I invoke the considerate judgment of mankind, and the gracious favor of Almighty God.

In witness whereof, I have hereunto set my hand and caused the seal of the United States to be affixed.

Done at the City of Washington, this first day of January, in the year of our Lord one thousand eight hundred and sixty three, and of the Independence of the United States of America the eighty-seventh.

By the President: ABRAHAM LINCOLN
WILLIAM H. SEWARD, Secretary of State.

The Emancipation Proclamation is a paradoxical document. Although he had no constitutional right to do so, Lincoln declared the slaves free in areas that had declared themselves free of his presidential influence; and he made no declaration of freedom for slaves in areas loyal to the Union or already conquered by Union armed forces. Only states in a state of rebellion were affected, and until conquered not even they were. Yet the declaration was the hallmark of Lincoln's presidency, made him the Great Liberator, and secured his special place in American history, the American memory, and the American mind.

LINCOLN'S DEEPEST MOTIVES: THE BURLINGAME THESIS CONTINUED

While Lincoln's earliest actions showed little evidence that he considered it his duty or right to free the slaves, he had by 1854 begun to speak vocally and equivocally against slavery, not only against its extension westward but against its very existence, calling slavery a "monster," a "moral, social, and political evil," a "monstrous injustice," and the "sum of all villainies."

The Great Emancipator, 1864, Abraham Lincoln as he would be most remembered, the man who saved the Union and freed the slaves. This photograph by Matthew Brady would become the model for future Lincoln images.

Historian Michael Burlingame, who explained Lincoln's mid-life crisis, believes he knows why Lincoln developed such a personal distaste for slavery. In a chapter of his *Inner World of Abraham Lincoln* titled "I Used to be a Slave," he attributes this distaste to the way Lincoln interpreted his own early life in his father's house. As Lincoln once said in a speech in Illinois: "We were all slaves one time or another. . . . I used to be a slave, and now I am so free that they let me practice law."

Burlingame sees great significance in such comments by Lincoln. Here is another: "When I see strong hands sowing, reaping, and threshing wheat and those same hands grinding and making that wheat into bread, I cannot refrain from wishing, and believing, that those hands, someway, in God's good time, shall own the mouth they feed." Burlingame postulates that Lincoln here may have been seeing in the life of a slave his own young self.

> As a youth, Lincoln was like a slave to his father, who insisted that his son not only labor on the family farm but also that he work for neighbors and then turn over every penny that he had earned. Soon after Lincoln started school in Indiana, Thomas Lincoln removed him and set him to work for neighbors in order to help solve Thomas's financial problems and perhaps to thwart the boy's interest in reading. No direct evidence illuminates Lincoln's feelings about being forced to work hard and then turn over all the earnings to his father, but an anecdote from his presidential years is suggestive. One day during the Civil War he described the joy he felt at earning his first money, a whole dollar given him for rowing two men from a riverbank to a steamboat. "I could scarcely credit that I, the poor boy, had earned a dollar in less than a day; that by honest work I had earned a dollar. The world seemed wider and fairer before me; I was a more hopeful and thoughtful boy from that time. It was, perhaps, the first money that he had earned without being leased out by his father and thus could keep; his obvious delight indicates that it may have been. . . .

> Lincoln's relationship with his father was chilly. Much evidence supports [historian] Richard N. Current's[4] conclusion that "there must have been a real estrangement" between the two. Lincoln's cousin, Dennis Hanks, who lived with the Lincoln family from the time Abraham was seven, doubted whether "Abe Loved his father very well or Not," and concluded "I Don[']t think he Did." Although a relatively placid, easy-going man, Thomas Lincoln could treat his son with "great barbarity," according to Hanks's son-in-law. Hanks testified that Thomas Lincoln would sometimes "slash" his boy for reading instead of doing chores. Hanks also recalled other episodes of physical abuse: "When strangers would ride along and up to his father's

---

[4] Current is author of several books on Lincoln as well as editor of *The Encyclopedia of the Confederacy.*

fence, Abe always, through pride and to tease his father, would be sure to ask the stranger the first question, for which his father would sometimes knock him a rod. . . . Abe, when whipped by his father, never balked, but dropped a kind of silent unwelcome tear.

[Lincoln's first cousin] Sophie Hanks, who lived with the Lincolns in Indiana, recalled that rather than whipping Abraham in front of guests, Tom Lincoln would wait until they had gone and then deal with the boy. She told her children that one morning a poor, usually barefoot neighbor named Jenkins called on Tom Lincoln. When young Abe saw him, he said, "Hello, Mr. Jenkins. You are doing better than you used to. You have a new pair of boots." Tom Lincoln took his boy inside a "gave Abe a little drilling" because his remarks might have offended Jenkins. " 'Well,' said Abe, 'he's got the boots.' " According to her son, Sophie Hanks "always said that the worst trouble with Abe was when people was talking—if they said something that wasn't right Abe would up and tell them so. Uncle Tom had a hard time to break him of this. She also recalled how Lincoln "very often would correct his father in talking when his father was telling how anything happened and if he didn[']t get it jest right or left out any thing, Abe would but[t] in right there and correct it." This recollection was borne out by Lincoln's stepmother, who related how he once challenged his father's version of a story, saying "Paw, that was not jest the way it was." For this act of lese-majeste, Tom slapped Abe in the face. As the Lincolns prepared to leave Indiana for Illinois, Jimmy Grigsby observed Thomas Lincoln impatiently awaiting his tardy son. When Abraham finally arrived, his father, carrying an ox whip, approached him. Grigsby then whispered to a friend, "Watch old Tom flail him." But instead the elder Lincoln handed his son the whip and told him to lead the procession. . . .

The source of Tom Lincoln's attitude may in part have been Abraham's distaste for farm work. "Farming, grubbing, hoeing, [and] making fences" held no charm for the boy, according to his cousin John Hanks. His stepmother told Herndon that "Abe was a good boy," but "he didn't like physical labor." Abraham often worked for a neighbor, who recalled that the boy "was always reading and thinking, (so) I used to get mad at him. . . . I say Abe was awful lazy. [H]e would laugh and talk and crack jokes and tell stories all the time. . . . Lincoln said to me one day that his father taught him to work but never learned him to love it."

Thomas Lincoln scarcely tolerated his boy's obsession with learning. John B. Helm stated that the father of the future president "looked upon bone and muscle [as] sufficient to make the man and that time spent in school as doubly wasted." To discourage the reading habit, Thomas used to conceal Abraham's books and sometimes even threw them away. According to Sarah Bush Johnston Lincoln, her husband "was not easily reconciled" to the suggestion that young Abraham be allowed to attend school and to read at home, but in time he relented.

Five years after Abraham had struck out on his own at the age of twenty-two, Thomas Lincoln told William G. Greene, "I suppose that Abe is still fooling hisself with eddication. I tried to stop it, but he has got that fool idea in his head, and it can't be got out. Now I hain't got no eddication, but I get along far better than ef I had." At that point Thomas Lincoln demonstrated how he kept accounts by marking a rafter with a piece of coal and then proudly remarked, "That thar's a heap better'n yer eddication." He added that "if Abe don't fool away all his time on his books, he may make something yet."

When Thomas tried to instruct Abraham in his own trade of carpentry, the boy demonstrated so little interest that the effort was soon abandoned. He was equally unenthusiastic about his father's favorite leisure pursuits, hunting and fishing, partly because of his tender feelings for animals. Those feelings were not strong enough, however, to keep him from deliberately killing one of his father's dogs. That may have been an act of unconscious revenge for Thomas's slaughter of young Abraham's pet pig, to which the boy had been devoted.

By the time he was nineteen, Abraham had grown so alienated that he seriously considered running away from home, even though the law required him to stay there and obey his father's command until he reached his majority. After returning from his first trip to New Orleans and handing over all the money he had earned to his father, Lincoln visited William Wood and said, "I want you to go to the river and give me a recommendation to some boat. I want a start." Wood refused, saying, "Abe, your age is against you. You're not twenty-one. I won't do it for your own good." . . .

Three years after he had asked William Wood help him to escape home, Lincoln fled the quasi-slavery he endured at the hands of his father and drifted off to New Salem; thereafter he had little to do with Thomas Lincoln. When his law practice took him to Coles County, as it occasionally did in the 1840s, Lincoln as a rule stayed at the home of his cousin Dennis Hanks or at the Union Hotel rather than at his father's house. Although he helped his father financially now and then, he did so seldom and grudgingly. Also surprising is Lincoln's reluctance to name a son after his father until after Thomas's death. Mary and Abraham Lincoln named their first boy after her father, Robert Todd; their second after Lincoln's friend, Edward D. Baker; and their third after Mrs. Lincoln's brother-in-law, William Wallace. Only the fourth and final son, born two years after Thomas Lincoln died, was given his name. Even so, Lincoln never called this boy Thomas or Tom, but rather Tad.

When notified in 1851 that his father lay dying, Lincoln refused to make the relatively short journey to honor his father's request that they say farewell. Coldly he instructed his stepbrother to tell Thomas "that if we could meet now, it is doubtful whether it would not be more painful than pleasant." When the old man died shortly afterward, Lincoln did not attend the funeral, nor did he have the gravesite marked with a stone.

WHITE REACTIONS TO THE EMANCIPATION PROCLAMATION

Not surprisingly, the Emancipation Proclamation brought forth strong reactions. Free blacks and runaway slaves swelled the ranks of the Union army and helped win the war because they realized a Union victory would secure freedom for all. While not all Northern whites applauded—Lincoln's own state of Illinois saw official protests of it—strong abolitionists were unanimous in their praise. Senator Charles Sumner of Massachusetts, who had urged Lincoln to act decisively from the beginning of the war, heaped high praise on the president and called it the "cornerstone of our national policy" from that time on. Speaking at Boston's Faneuil Hall on October 6, 1862, in response to the first draft of September 22, Sumner said:

> Thank God that I live to enjoy this day! Thank God that my eyes have not closed without seeing this great salvation! The skies are brighter and the air is purer now that Slavery is handed over to judgment.
>
> By the proclamation of the President, all persons held as slaves January 1, 1863, within any State or designated part of a State, the people whereof shall then be in rebellion against the United States, shall be then, thenceforward, and forever free; and the Executive Government of the United States, including the military and naval authority thereof, will recognize and maintain the freedom of such persons, and will do no act or acts to repress such persons, or any of them, in any efforts they may make for their actual freedom. Beyond these most effective words, which do not go into operation before the new year, are other words of immediate operation, constituting a present edict of Emancipation. The President recites the recent Acts of Congress applicable to this question, and calls upon all persons in the military and naval service to observe, obey, and enforce them. But these Acts provide that all slaves of Rebels, taking refuge within the liens of our army, all slaves captured from Rebels or deserted by them, and all slaves found in any place occupied by Rebel forces and afterwards occupied by forces of the United States, shall be forever free of servitude, and not again held as slaves; and these Acts further provide that no person in the military or naval service shall,

under any pretence whatever, assume to decide on the validity of any claim to a slave, or surrender any such person to his claimant, on pain of being dismissed from the service: so that by these Acts, now proclaimed by the President, Freedom is practically secured to all who find shelter within our lines, and the glorious flag of the Union, wherever it floats, becomes the flag of Freedom. . . .

And now, thank God, the word is spoken!—greater word was seldom spoken. Emancipation has begun, and our country is already elevated and glorified. The war has not changed in object, but it has changed in character. Its object now, as at the beginning, is simply to put down the Rebellion; but its character is derived from the new force at length enlisted, stamping itself upon all that is done, and absorbing the whole war to itself. Vain will it be again to delude European nations into foolish belief that Slavery has nothing to do with the war, that it is a war for empire on one side and independence on the other, and that all generous ideas are on the side of the Rebellion. And vain, also, will be that other European cry,—whether from an intemperate press or the cautious lips of statesmen,—that separation is inevitable, and that our Government is doomed to witness the dismemberment of the Republic. With this new alliance, such forbodings will be falsified, the wishes of the fathers will be fulfilled, and the rights of human nature, which were the declared object of our Revolution, vindicated. Thus inspired, the sword of Washington—that sword which, according to his last will and testament, was to be drawn only in self-defence, or in defence of country and its rights—will once more marshal our armies to victory, while the national flag, wherever it floats, will give freedom to all beneath its folds, and the proud inscription be at last triumphantly verified: "Liberty and Union, now and forever, one and inseparable."

But, fellow-citizens, the war we wage is not merely for ourselves, it is for all mankind. Slavery yet lingers in Brazil, and beneath the Spanish flag in those two golden possessions, Cuba and Porto Rico; but nowhere can it survive extinction here. Therefore we conquer for Liberty everywhere. In ending Slavery here we open its gates all over the world, and let the oppressed go free. Nor is this all. In saving the Republic we save Civilization. Man throughout his long pilgrimage on earth has been compelled to suffer much, but Slavery is the heaviest burden he has been called to bear: It is the only burden our country has been called to bear. Let it drop, and this happy republic, with humanity in its train, all changed in raiment and in countenance, like the Christian Pilgrim, will hurry upward to the celestial gate. If thus far our example has failed, it is simply because of Slavery. Vain to proclaim our unparalleled prosperity, the comfort diffused among a numerous people, resources without stint, or even the education of our children; the enemies of the Republic had but to say, "There is slavery," and our example became powerless. But let

Slavery disappear, and the same example will be of irresistible might. Without firing a gun or writing a dispatch, it will revolutionize the world.

A very different reaction, not unexpectedly, came from the president of the Confederacy, Jefferson Davis. Born in Kentucky, as was Lincoln, Davis, who had been a Democratic senator from Mississippi and U.S. secretary of war under President Franklin Pierce, now represented the secessionist slave states that were the target of Lincoln's proclamation. With the following words Davis, addressing a joint session of the Senate and House of Representatives of the Confederate States of America in Richmond on January 21, 1863, responded to the official proclamation.

The public journals of the North have been received, containing a proclamation, dated on the 1st day of the present month, signed by the President of the United States, in which he orders and declares all slaves within ten of the States of the Confederacy to be free, except such as are found within certain districts now occupied in part by the armed forces of the enemy. We may well leave it to the instincts of that common humanity which a beneficent Creator has implanted in the breasts of our fellowmen of all countries to pass judgement on a measure by which several millions of human beings of an inferior race, peaceful and contended laborers in their sphere, are doomed to extermination, while at the same time they are encouraged to a general assassination of their masters by the insidious recommendation "to abstain from violence unless in necessary self-defense." Our own detestation of those who have attempted the most execrable measure recorded in the history of guilty man is tempered by profound contempt for the impotent rage which it discloses. So far as regards the action of this Government on such criminals as may attempt its execution, I confine myself to informing you that I shall, unless in your wisdom you deem some other course more expedient, deliver to the several State authorities all commissioned officers of the United States that may hereafter be captured by our forces in any of the States embraced in the proclamation, that they may be dealt within in accordance with the laws of those States providing for the punishment of criminals engaged in exciting servile insurrection. The enlisted soldiers I shall continue to treat as unwilling instruments in the commission of these crimes, and shall direct their discharge and return to their homes on the proper and usual parole.

In its political aspect this measure possesses great significance, and to it in this light I invite your attention. It affords to our whole people the complete and crowning proof of the true nature of the designs of the party which elevated to power the present occupant of the Presidential chair at Washington and which sought to conceal its purpose by every variety of artful device and by the perfidious use of the most solemn and repeated pledges on every possible occasion. . . .

Both before and after the actual commencement of hostilities the President of the United States repeated in formal official communication to the Cabinets of Great Britain and France that he was utterly without constitutional power to do the act which he has just committed, and that in no possible event, whether the secession of these States resulted in the establishment of a separate Confederacy or in the restoration of the Union, was there any authority by virtue of which he could either restore a disaffected State to the Union by force of arms or make any change in any of its institutions. I refer especially for verification of this assertion to the dispatches addressed by the Secretary of State of the United States, under direction of the President, to the Ministers of the United States at London and Paris, under date of 10th and 22d of April, 1861.

The people of this Confederacy, then, cannot fail to receive this proclamation as the fullest vindication of their own sagacity in forseeing the uses to which the dominant party in the United States intended from the beginning to apply their power, nor can they cease to remember with devout thankfulness that it is to their own vigilance in resisting the first stealthy progress of approaching despotism that they owe their escape from consequences now apparent to the most skeptical. This proclamation will have another salutary effect in calming the fears of those who have constantly evinced the apprehension that this war might end by some reconstruction of the Old Union or some renewal of close political relations with the United States. These fears have never been shared by me, nor have I ever been able to perceive on what basis they could rest. But the proclamation affords the fullest guarantee of the impossibility of such a result; it has established a state of things which can lead to but one of three possible consequences—the extermination of the slaves, the exile of the whole white population from the Confederacy, or absolute and total separation of these States from the United States.

This proclamation is also an authentic statement by the Government of the United States of its inability to subjugate the South by force of arms, and as such must be accepted by neutral nations, which can no longer find any justification in withholding our just claims to formal recognition. It is also in effect an intimation to the people of the North that they must prepare to submit to a separation, now become inevitable, for that people are too acute not to understand a restoration of the Union has been rendered forever impossible by the adoption of a measure which from its very nature neither admits or retraction nor can coexist with union.

AFRICAN-AMERICAN RESPONSES TO THE EMANCIPATION PROCLAMATION

The response of most African Americans to the Emancipation Proclamation was immediate and jubilant. Celebrations were held in black communities across the North, and free black men began joining the Union army in great numbers. Their presence may have been the decisive factor in a number of victories, even, some historians say, in the outcome of the war. But as the years passed some black leaders raised questions, amid continuing general approval, about Lincoln's overall performance as president during the great crisis.

Frederick Douglass (1876)

Frederick Douglass, speaking at a dedication of the Freedmen's Monument on July 4, 1875, was truthful about the mixed feelings of some black people toward Lincoln and the proclamation. Douglass had been a friend of Lincoln, and he felt he could express himself freely about the man he still believed was "the first martyr President of the United States." Douglass, himself free long before the Civil War and an abolitionist long before Lincoln was elected president, was nothing like the humble black man of the stone monument being dedicated, who knelt before a kindly Lincoln, thanking him for his freedom.

> Fellow-citizens, in what we have said and done to-day, and in what we may say and do hereafter, we disclaim everything like arrogance and assumption. We claim for ourselves no superior devotion to the character, history, and memory of the illustrious name whose monument we have here dedicated to-day. We fully comprehend the relation of Abraham Lincoln both to ourselves and to the white people of the United States. Truth is proper and beautiful at all times and in all places, and it is never more proper and beautiful in any case than when speaking of a great public man whose example is likely to be commended for honor and imitation long after his departure to the solemn shades, the silent continents of eternity. It must be admitted, truth compels me to admit, even here in the presence of the monument we have erected to his memory, Abraham Lincoln was not, in the fullest sense of the word, either our man or our model. In his interests, in his associations, in his habits of thought, and in his prejudices, he was a white man.
>
> He was pre-eminently the white man's President, entirely devoted to the welfare of white men. He was ready and willing at any

time during the first years of his administration to deny, postpone, and sacrifice the rights of humanity in the colored people to promote the welfare of the white people of this country. In all his education and feeling he was an American of the Americans. He came into the Presidential chair upon one principle alone, namely, opposition to the extension of slavery. His arguments in furtherance of this policy had their motive and mainspring in his patriotic devotion to the interests of his own race. To protect, defend, and perpetuate slavery in the States where it existed Abraham Lincoln was not less ready than any other President to draw the sword of the nation. He was ready to execute all the supposed constitutional guarantees of the United States Constitution in favor of the slave system anywhere inside the slave States. He was willing to pursue, recapture, and send back the fugitive slave to his master, and to suppress a slave rising for liberty, though his guilty master were already in arms against the Government. The race to which we belong were not the special objects of his consideration. Knowing this, I concede to you, my white fellow-citizens, a pre-eminence in this worship at once full and supreme. First, midst, and last, you and yours were the objects of his deepest affection and his most earnest solicitude. You are the children of Abraham Lincoln. We are at best only his step-children; children by adoption, children by force of circumstances and necessity. To you it especially belongs to sound his praises, to preserve and perpetuate his memory, to multiply his statues, to hang his pictures high upon your walls, and commend his example, for to you he was a great and glorious friend and benefactor. Instead of supplanting you at this altar, we would exhort you to build high his monuments; let them be of the most costly material, of the most cunning workmanship; let their forms be symmetrical, beautiful, and perfect; let their bases be upon solid rocks, and their summits lean against the unchanging blue, overhanging sky, and let them endure forever! But while in the abundance of your wealth, and in the fatness of your just and patriotic devotion, you do all this, we entreat you to despise not the humble offering we this day unveil to view; for while Abraham Lincoln saved for you a country, he delivered us from a bondage, according to Jefferson, one hour of which was worse than ages of the oppression your fathers rose in rebellion to oppose. . . .

I have said that President Lincoln was a white man, and shared the prejudices common to his countrymen towards the colored race. Looking back to his times and to the condition of his country, we are compelled to admit that this unfriendly feeling on his part may be safely set down as one element of his wonderful success in organizing the loyal American people for the tremendous conflict before them, and bringing them safely through that conflict. His great mission was to accomplish two things: first, to save his country from dismemberment and ruin; and second, to free his country from the great crime of slavery. To do one or the other, or both, he must have the earnest sympathy and the powerful co-operation of his loyal fellow-countrymen. Without this primary and essential condition to success his efforts must have been vain and utterly fruitless. Had he put the abolition of slavery before the salvation of the Union, he would have inevitably driven from him a powerful class of the American people and rendered resistance to rebellion impossible. Viewed from the genuine abolition ground, Mr. Lincoln seemed tardy, cold, dull, and indifferent; but measuring him by the sentiment of his country, a sentiment he was bound as a statesman to consult, he was swift, zealous, radical, and determined.

Though Mr. Lincoln shared the prejudices of his white fellow-countrymen against the negro, it is hardly necessary to say that in his heart of hearts he loathed and hated slavery. The man who could say, "Fondly do we hope, fervently do we pray, that this mighty scourge of war shall soon pass away, yet if God wills it continue till all the wealth piled by two hundred years of bondage shall have been wasted, and each drop of blood drawn by the lash shall have been paid for by one drawn by the sword, the judgments of the Lord are true and righteous altogether," gives all needed proof of his feeling on the subject of slavery. He was willing, while the South was loyal, that it should have its pound of flesh, because he thought that it was so nominated in the bond; but farther than this no earthly power could make him go. . . .

Happily for the country, happily for you and for me, the judgment of James Buchanan[5], the patrician, was not the judgment of Abraham Lincoln, the plebeian. He brought his strong common sense, sharpened in the school of adversity, to bear upon the question. He did not hesitate, he did not doubt, he did not falter; but at once resolved that at whatever peril, at whatever cost, the union of the States should be preserved. A patriot himself, his faith was strong and unwavering in the patriotism of his countrymen. Timid men said before Mr. Lincoln's inauguration, that we had seen the last President of the United States. A voice in influential quarters said "Let the Union slide." Some said that a Union maintained by the sword was worthless. Others said a rebellion of 8,000,000 cannot be suppressed; but in the midst of all this tumult and timidity, and against all this, Abraham Lincoln was clear in his duty, and had an oath in heaven. He calmly and bravely heard the voice of doubt and fear all around him; but he had an oath in heaven, and there was not power enough on the earth to make this honest boatman, back-woodsman, and broad-handed splitter of rails evade or violate that sacred oath. He had not been schooled in the ethics of slavery; his plain life had favored his love of truth. He had not been taught that treason and perjury were the proof of honor and honesty. His moral training was against his saying one thing when he meant

---

[5] Buchanan was Lincoln's predecessor in the White House.

another. The trust which Abraham Lincoln had in himself and in the people was surprising and grand, but it was also enlightened and well founded. He knew the American people better than they knew themselves, and his truth was based upon this knowledge.

Had Abraham Lincoln died from any of the numerous ills to which flesh is heir; had he reached that good old age of which his vigorous constitution and his temperate habits gave promise; had he been permitted to see the end of his great work; had the solemn curtain of death come down but gradually—we should still have been smitten with a heavy grief, and treasured his name lovingly. But dying as he did die, by the red hand of violence, killed, assassinated, taken off without warning, not because of personal hate—for no man who knew Abraham Lincoln could hate him—but because of his fidelity to union and liberty, he is doubly dear to us, and his memory will be precious forever.

Booker T. Washington (1909)

Some of Douglass's comments seemed to embarrass President Grant, Lincoln's leading general during the war, who attended the dedication. Grant would probably not have been embarrassed, had he been present, by the following words of turn-of-the-century black leader Booker T. Washington, although Washington's words of tribute to Lincoln did include a few subtle reminders of black reservations. Washington, founder of Alabama's Tuskegee Institute, which he hoped would train black Americans for the day they would take their place as equal citizens, spoke these words at the Republican Club in New York City on Lincoln's birthday 1909.

Mr. Chairman, Ladies and Gentlemen: You ask that which he found a piece of property and turned into a free American citizen to speak to you tonight on Abraham Lincoln. I am not fitted by ancestry or training to be your teacher tonight for, as I have stated, I was born a slave.

My first knowledge of Abraham Lincoln came in this way: I was awakened early one morning before the dawn of day, as I lay wrapped in a bundle of rags on the dirt floor of our slave cabin, by the prayers of my mother, just before leaving for her day's work, as she was kneeling over my body earnestly praying that Abraham Lincoln might succeed, and that one day she and her boy might be free. You give me the opportunity here this evening to celebrate with you and the nation the answer to that prayer.

Says the Great Book somewhere, "Though a man die, yet shall he live." If this is true of the ordinary man, how much more true is it of the hero of the hour and the hero of the century—Abraham Lincoln! One hundred years of the life and influence of Lincoln is the story of the struggles, the trials, ambitions, and triumphs of the people of our complex American civilization. Interwoven into the warp and woof of this human complexity is the moving story of men and women of nearly every race and color in their progress from slavery to freedom, from poverty to wealth, from weakness to power, from ignorance to intelligence. Knit into the life of Abraham Lincoln is the story and success of the nation in the blending of all tongues, religions, colors, races into one composite nation, leaving each group and race free to live its own separate social life, and yet all a part of the great whole.

If a man die, shall he live? Answering this question as applied to our martyred President, perhaps you expect me to confine my words of appreciation to the great boon which, through him, was conferred upon my race. My undying gratitude and that of ten millions of my race for this and yet more! To have been the instrument used by Providence through which four millions of slaves, now grown into ten millions of free citizens, were made free would bring eternal fame within itself, but this is not the only claim that Lincoln has upon our sense of gratitude and appreciation. . . .

The signing of the Emancipation Proclamation was a great event, and yet it was but the symbol of another, still greater and more momentous. We who celebrate this anniversary should not forget that the same pen that gave freedom to four millions of African slaves at the same time struck the shackles from the souls of twenty-seven millions of Americans of another color.

In any country, regardless of what its laws say, wherever people act upon the idea that the disadvantage of one man is the good of another, there slavery exists. Wherever in any country the whole people feel that the happiness of all is dependent upon the happiness of the weakest, there freedom exists.

In abolishing slavery, Lincoln proclaimed the principle that, even in the case of the humblest and weakest of mankind, the welfare of each is still the good of all. In reestablishing in this country the principle that, at bottom, the interests of humanity and of the individual are one, he freed men's souls from spiritual bondage, he freed them to mutual helpfulness. Henceforth no man of any race, either in the North or in the South, need feel constrained to fear or hate his brother.

By the same token that Lincoln made America free, he pushed back the boundaries of freedom everywhere, gave the spirit of liberty a wider influence throughout the world, and reestablished the dignity of man as man.

By the same act that freed my race, he said to the civilized and uncivilized world that man everywhere must be free, and that man everywhere must be enlightened, and the Lincoln spirit of freedom and fair play will never cease to spread and grow in power till throughout the world all men shall know the truth, and the truth shall make them free.

Lincoln in his day was wise enough to recognize that which is true in the present and for all time: that in a state of slavery and ignorance man renders the lowest and most costly form of service to his fellows. In a state of freedom and enlightenment he renders the highest and most helpful form of service. . . .

As a race we are learning, I believe, in an increasing degree that the best way for us to honor the memory of our Emancipator is by seeking to imitate him. Like Lincoln, the Negro race should seek to be simple, without bigotry and without ostentation. There is great power in simplicity. We as a race should, like Lincoln, have moral courage to be what we are, and not pretend to be what we are not. We should keep in mind that no one can degrade us except ourselves; that if we are worthy, no influence can defeat us. Like other races, the Negro will often meet obstacles, often be sorely tried and tempted; but we must keep in mind that freedom, in the broadest and highest sense, has never been a bequest; it has been a conquest. In the final test, the success of our race will be in proportion to the service that it renders to the world. In the long run, the badge of service is the badge of sovereignty.

   With all his other elements of strength, Abraham Lincoln possessed in the highest degree patience and, as I have said, courage. The highest form of courage is not always that exhibited on the battlefield in the midst of the blare of trumpets and the waving of banners. The highest courage is of the Lincoln kind. It is the same kind of courage, made possible by the new life and the new possibilities furnished by Lincoln's Proclamation, displayed by thousands of men and women of my race every year who are going out from Tuskegee and other Negro institutions in the South to lift up their fellows. When they go, often into lonely and secluded districts, with little thought of salary, with little thought of personal welfare, no drums beat, no banners fly, no friends stand by to cheer them on; but these brave young souls who are erecting schoolhouses, creating school systems, prolonging school terms, teaching the people to buy homes, build houses, and live decent lives are fighting the battles of this country just as truth and bravery as any persons who go forth to fight battles against a foreign foe. . . .

Lincoln lives today because he had the courage which made him refuse to hate the man at the South or the man at the North when they did not agree with him. He had the courage as well as the patience and foresight to suffer in silence, to be misunderstood, to be abused, to refuse to revile when reviled. For he knew that, if he was right, the ridicule of today would be the applause of tomorrow. He knew, too, that at some time in the distant future our nation would repent of the folly of cursing our public servants while they live and blessing them only when they die. In this connection I cannot refrain from suggesting the question to the millions of voices raised today in his praise: "Why did you not say it yesterday?" Yesterday, when one word of approval and gratitude would have meant so much to him in strengthening his hand and heart. . . .

As we gather here, brothers all, in common joy and thanksgiving for the life of Lincoln, may I not ask that you, the worthy representatives of seventy millions of white Americans, join heart and hand with the ten millions of black Americans—these ten millions who speak your tongue, profess your religion—who have never lifted their voices or hands except in defense of their country's honor and their country's flag—and swear eternal fealty to the memory and the traditions of the sainted Lincoln? I repeat, may we not join with your race, and let all of us here highly resolve that justice, good will, and peace shall be the motto of our lives? If this be true, in the highest sense Lincoln shall not have lived and died in vain.

TWENTIETH-CENTURY ASSESSMENTS OF THE EMANCIPATION PROCLAMATION

Analysis and assessment of the Emancipation Proclamation began within a few months of its emotional reception. The speech by Frederick Douglass in 1876 was one of the earliest and clearest public judgements. That of Booker T. Washington in 1909 followed in this tradition. Countless scholars as well have examined and explained the historical, political, and social significance of the Emancipation Proclamation. The following two recent assessments, by John Hope Franklin and by Stephen B. Oates, are among the best. Both Franklin and Oates consider Lincoln more principled and his motives more honorable than do many historians who see the proclamation as a gesture by a man of weak convictions to gain the upper hand in the struggle to win the war.

John Hope Franklin

John Hope Franklin, an African American historian, is author of *Color and Racism, Black Leaders of the Twentieth Century,* and *From Slavery to Freedom: A History of African Americans.* The following excerpt is from his book *The Emancipation Proclamation.*

Both by what it said and what it did not say, the Proclamation greatly contributed to the significant shift in 1863 in the way the war was regarded. It recognized the right of emancipated slaves to defend their freedom. The precise language was that they should "abstain from all violence, unless in necessary self-defence." It also provided that former slaves could now be received into the armed services. While it was clear that they were to fight to save the Union, the fact remained that since their own fate was tied to that of the Union, they would also be fighting for their own freedom. The Negro who, in December 1862, could salute his own colonel instead of blacking the boots of a Confederate colonel, as he had been doing a year earlier, had a stake in the war that was not difficult to define. However loyal to the Union the Negro troops were—and they numbered some 190,000 by April 1865—one is inclined to believe that they were fighting primarily for freedom for themselves and their brothers in the months that followed the issuance of the Emancipation Proclamation.

Despite the fact that the President laid great stress on the issuance of the Proclamation as a military necessity, he did not entirely overlook the moral and humanitarian significance of the measure. And even in the document itself he gave some indication of his appreciation of this particular dimension that was, in time, to eclipse many other considerations. He said that the emancipation of the slaves was "sincerely believed to be an act of justice." This conception of emancipation could hardly be confined to the slaves in states or parts of states that were in rebellion against the United States on January 1, 1863. It must be recalled, moreover, that in the same sentence that he referred to emancipation as an "act of justice" he invoked "the considerate judgment of mankind and the gracious favor of Almighty God." This raised the Proclamation above the level of just another measure for the effective prosecution of the war. And, in turn, the war became more than a war to save the integrity and independence of the Union. It became also a war to promote the freedom of mankind. . . .

Slavery, in or out of the Confederacy, could not possibly have survived the Emancipation Proclamation. Slaves themselves, already restive under their yoke and walking off the plantation in many places, were greatly encouraged upon learning that Lincoln wanted them to be free. They proceeded to oblige him. There followed what one authority has called a general strike and another has described as widespread slave disloyalty throughout the confederacy. Lincoln understood the full implications of the Proclamation. That is one of the reasons why he delayed issuing it as long as he did. Once the power of the government was enlisted on the side of freedom in one place, it could not successfully be restrained from supporting freedom in some other place. It was too fine a distinction to make. Not even the slaveholders in the excepted areas could make it. They knew, therefore, that the Emancipation Proclamation was the beginning of the end of slavery for them. Many of them did not like it, but the realities of the situation clearly indicated what the future had in store for them. . . .

Despite the fact that the immediate results of the Emancipation Proclamation were not always measurable, Lincoln was pleased with what he had done. Over and over again he expressed the view that he had done the right thing. It had not had an adverse effect on the course of the war. The war, he told a correspondent in the summer of 1863, had "certainly progressed as favorably for us, since the issue of the proclamation as before." The Proclamation was valid, and he would never retract it. Moreover, it reflected his own repugnance to slavery. As an antislavery man, he wrote Major General Nathanial P. Banks, he had a motive for issuing the Proclamation that went beyond military considerations. At last he had been able to strike the blow for freedom that he had long wanted to do.

Finally, Lincoln hoped that the Proclamation would provide the basis for a new attitude and policy for Negroes. That all slaves would soon be free was a reality that all white men should face. "Those who shall have tasted actual freedom I believe can never be slaves, or quasi slaves again." He hoped, therefore, that the several states would adopt some practical system "by which the two races could gradually live themselves out of their old relation to each other, and both come out better prepared for the new." He hoped that states would provide for the education of Negroes, and he went so far as to suggest to Governor Michael Hahn of Louisiana that this state might consider extending the franchise to free Negroes of education and property.

Thus, in many ways the Proclamation affected the course of the war as well as Lincoln's way of thinking about the problem of Negroes in the United States. Abroad, it rallied large numbers of people to the North's side and became a valuable instrument of American foreign policy. At home it sharpened the issues of the war and provided a moral and humanitarian ingredient that had been lacking. It fired the leaders with a new purpose and gave to the President a new weapon. Small wonder that he no longer promoted the idea of colonization. Small wonder that he began to advocate education and the franchise for Negroes. They were a new source of strength that deserved to be treated as the loyal citizens that they were.

For the last hundred years the Emancipation Proclamation has maintained its place as one of America's truly important documents. Even when the principles it espoused were not universally endorsed and even when its beneficiaries were the special target of mistreatment of one kind or another, the Proclamation somehow retained its hold on the very people who saw its promises unfulfilled. It did not do this because of the perfection of the goal to which it aspired. At best it sought to save the Union by freeing *some* of the slaves. Nor did it do it by the sublimity of its language. It had neither the felicity of the Declaration of Independence nor the simple grandeur of the Gettysburg Address. But in a very real sense it was another step toward the extension of the ideal of equality about which Jefferson had written.

Lincoln wrote the Emancipation Proclamation amid severe psychological and legal handicaps. Unlike Jefferson, whose Declaration of Independence was a clean break with a legal and constitutional system that had hitherto restricted thought and action, Lincoln was compelled to forge a document of freedom for the slaves within the existing constitutional system and in a manner that would give even greater support to that constitutional system. This required not only courage and daring but considerable ingenuity as well. As in so many of Lincoln's acts the total significance and validity of the measure were not immediately apparent, even among those who were sympathetic with its aims. Gradually, the greatness of the document dawned upon the nation and the world. Gradually, it took its place with the great documents of human freedom.

Stephen B. Oates

Stephen B. Oates, whose analysis of events leading to the issuance of the proclamation have been presented, is author of *With Malice Toward None* and *Abraham Lincoln: The Man Behind the Myths*. This excerpt is from "A Momentous Decree," a paper presented at a symposium on Lincoln held in 1984, on the 175th anniversary of his birth.

We now know that Lincoln issued his proclamation for a combination of reasons: to clarify the status of the fugitive slaves, to solve the Union's manpower woes, to keep Great Britain out of the conflict, to maim and cripple the Confederacy by destroying its labor force, to remove the very thing that had caused the war, and to break the chains of several million oppressed human beings and right America at last with her own ideals. . . . Lincoln was no reluctant emancipator: he struck at slavery within a year after the war had begun, and he did so for moral as well as for political and military reasons. As much as possible in his time, he wanted America to realize the promise of equality made in the Declaration of Independence, which was the foundation of his politics. Lincoln himself was fully aware of the significance of his proclamation. "If my name ever goes into history," he said, "it will be for this act." . . .

The proclamation was not some anemic document that in effect freed no slaves. By November 1864 the *Philadelphia North American* estimated that more than 1,300,000 blacks had been liberated by Lincoln's proclamation or "the events of the war." By war's end, all

3,500,000 slaves in the defeated Confederacy could claim freedom under Lincoln's proclamation and the victorious Union flag. In fact, the proclamation was their only claim to freedom until the ratification of the <u>Thirteenth Amendment in December 1865.</u>

What is more, the proclamation did something for Lincoln personally that has never been stressed enough. In truth, the story of emancipation could well be called the liberation of Abraham Lincoln. For in the process of granting freedom to the slaves, Lincoln also emancipated himself from a painful personal dilemma: his love for a political system that preserved an institution he hated. His proclamation now brought the private and the public Lincoln together: now the public statesman could vanquish a thing the private citizen had always detested, a thing that had long had "the power of making me miserable." Now the public statesman could destroy what he considered "a cruel wrong" that had always besmirched America's experiment in popular government, had always impeded her historic mission in the progress of human liberty in the world.

The proclamation also opened the army to black volunteers, and Northern free blacks and Southern ex-slaves enlisted as Union fighting men. As Lincoln said, "The colored population is the great available and yet unavailed of, force for restoring the Union." And he now availed himself of that force, on a scale unprecedented in America. In all, some 186,000 black troops—most of them emancipated slaves—served in Union forces on every major battle front, helping to liberate their brothers and sisters in bondage and to save the American experiment in popular government. As Lincoln observed, the blacks added enormous and indispensable strength to the Union war machine. Without them, it is doubtful that he could have won the war. . . .

After he issued the Emancipation Proclamation, Lincoln never again urged colonization in public—an eloquent silence, indicating that he had concluded that Dixie's whites and liberated blacks must somehow learn to live together. Yet there is a persistent misconception that Lincoln to the end of his life was a champion of colonization. That view rests exclusively on the 1892 autobiography of Union political general Benjamin F. Butler. In it, Butler claimed that in April 1865 Lincoln feared a race war in the South and still wanted to ship the blacks abroad. Not only is Butler a highly dubious witness, but there is not a scintilla of corroborative evidence to support his story, which [historian] Mark E. Neely, Jr.,[6] has recently exploded as "entirely a fantasy." There is not a single other source that quotes the president stating, in public or in private, that he still favored colonization.

---

[6] Neely is author of *The Last Best Hope of Earth* and editor of *The Abraham Lincoln Encyclopedia.*

In any case, such a stance would have been glaringly inconsistent with Lincoln's Gettysburg Address, which called for a new birth of freedom in America for blacks and whites alike. (Here, in fact, is the eloquent defense of liberty that critics have found lacking in the proclamation itself.) And a colonization stance would have been inconsistent, too, with Lincoln's appreciation of the indispensable role his black soldiers played in subduing the rebellion. No one of Lincoln's honesty and sense of fair play would enlist 186,000 black troops to save the Union and then advocate throwing them out of the country. He simply did not advocate that. Still, he needed some device during the war, some program that would pacify white Northerners and convince them that Southern blacks would not flock into their communities, but would remain in the South instead. What Lincoln worked out was a refugee system, installed by his adjutant general in occupied Dixie, which utilized blacks there in a variety of civilian and military pursuits. Then Republican propaganda went to work selling Northern whites on the system and the Emancipation Proclamation. See, the argument went, liberated blacks will not invade the North, but will stay in Dixie as free wage earners, learning to help themselves and our Union cause.

Even so, emancipation remained the most explosive and unpopular act of Lincoln's embattled presidency. In the Confederacy, newspapers pronounced him a "fiend" who wanted to incite a race war in Dixie; Jefferson Davis considered the proclamation "the most execrable measure recorded in the history of guilty man," and rebels everywhere vowed to fight all the harder against the monster who had issued it. In the North, thousands of Democrats revolted against the administration in 1863, denouncing Lincoln as an abolitionist dictator who had surrendered to radicalism. In the Midwest, dissident Democrats launched a peace movement to throw "the shrieking abolitionist faction" out of office and negotiate a peace with the Confederacy that would somehow restore the Union with slavery intact. With Democrats up in arms, a storm of anti-black, anti-Lincoln protest rolled over the land, whipping up race and draft riots in several cities. And there was trouble in the army as well. Correspondents who traveled with Union forces claimed that hardly one soldier in ten approved of emancipation; and some officers from the Midwest even resigned in protest.

Clearly Lincoln's generation did not regard the proclamation as a meaningless paper decree. The wonder, of course, is that Lincoln stuck by a measure that aroused such public indignation. But the president seemed intractable. He had made up his mind to smash the slave society of the rebel South and eliminate the moral wrong of black bondage, and no amount of public discontent, he indicated, was going to change his mind. With his sense of history, he was also concerned with the judgments of posterity. "In times like the present," he had warned Congress, "men should utter nothing for which they would not willingly be responsible through time and eternity."

Still, he wavered once—in August 1864, a time of unrelenting gloom for Lincoln, when his popularity had sunk so low that it seemed he could not be reelected. He confessed that maybe the country would no longer sustain a war for slave liberation, that maybe he should not pull the nation down a road it did not want to travel. On August 24, he decided to offer Jefferson Davis peace terms that excluded emancipation as a condition, vaguely suggesting that slavery would be adjusted later "by peaceful means." But the next day Lincoln changed his mind. With awakened resolution, he vowed to fight the war through to unconditional surrender and to stand by emancipation come what may. He had made his promise of freedom to the slaves, and he meant to keep it as long as he was in office.

Here surely is one of the glories of the Lincoln story: a troubled, visionary president contending with an aroused Northern opposition, a determined Southern foe, and his own uncertainties and self-doubts, and yet somehow finding the inner strength to overcome them all. After he won reelection, thanks to timely union victories and the folly of the Democrats in running a major general on a peace plank in the midst of civil war, Lincoln used all the powers and prestige of his office to get the present Thirteenth Amendment through a recalcitrant House of Representatives (the Senate had already passed it). Lincoln did so to protect his proclamation, for he worried that it might be nullified in the courts or thrown out by a later Congress or a subsequent administration. When the House adopted the amendment, by just three votes more than the required two-thirds majority, Lincoln pronounced it "a great moral victory" and "a King's cure" for the evils of slavery. When ratified by the states, the amendment would end human bondage everywhere in America. Lincoln pointed across the Potomac: "If the people over the river had behaved themselves, I could not have done what I have."

SUMMARY: PRESSURE AND COURAGE

Some observers said—and still say—that Lincoln issued the Emancipation Proclamation because of pressure from abolitionists, reports of a losing war, and fear of a failed presidency. Some said—and say—that he acted out of conviction that slavery was evil and out of courage that enabled him to perform above the level of all previous presidents. It would seem from the comments of his contemporaries and the assessments of historians that both opinions are at least partially true. The pressures were there, but so were the convictions and so was the courage.

Whether the Emancipation Proclamation was born of necessity or conviction, whether it was legal, wise, or effective, whatever its results, it created the Lincoln image. Abraham Lincoln was forever afterward the Great Liberator. The decision confirmed his greatness, as fully equal if not superior to that of George Washington. It gave him an even higher role than that of Washington in the unfolding American pageant. Washington was America's Moses, leading the nation out of bondage to freedom and independence. That left the next and more important role to Abraham Lincoln.

QUESTIONS FOR RESPONSIVE ESSAYS

1. Why was Lincoln so reluctant and so slow to free the slaves, when he obviously had never approved of slavery? Why did he reject, during his first year in the White House, the pleas of advisers to issue a proclamation of emancipation? Did his delay ultimately help or harm the cause of freedom for slaves? How did his thoughts about the subject change even during the year 1862?

2. Discuss the theory behind the article "I Used to be a Slave." Does it satisfactorily explain Lincoln's reason for hating slavery? Does it explain his plan for colonization? What questions would you ask the author if you could?

3. Compare and contrast the reactions of Jefferson Davis and Charles Sumner to the issuance of the Emancipation Proclamation. How do their attitudes prove that the war would have to continue to a military solution?

4. Compare the tributes to Lincoln the Liberator by Frederick Douglass and Booker T. Washington. How do they agree and disagree about Lincoln's achievement and its motivation? Which man's sentiments do you think best represented the feelings of African Americans during the first fifty years after freedom? Which best represents them today?

5. Compare the recent assessments of Lincoln's proclamation by John Hope Franklin and Stephen B. Oates. What new perspectives have been gained more than a century since it was issued? How are the Franklin and Oates conclusions like and unlike those of Sumner, Douglass, and Washington?

PART IV

Lincoln the Redeemer

Because his death came when it did, the way it did, Lincoln the man, Lincoln the president, Lincoln the liberator became something more. He became a figure of legend, of myth, even of religion. Waldo Braden, introducing his collection of speeches on Lincoln called *Building the Myth*, said about this interesting phenomenon:

> This redefinition of Lincoln's place in American thought, his swift transcendence from history into folklore . . . was the product of many influences, including religious fervor, superstition, the retrospective impact of Lincoln's own last public utterances, and popular art. Lincoln the man was swallowed by the myth, a myth neither the passage of time nor the challenge of revision has been able to tarnish.

From the very moment Lincoln died from an assassin's bullet, he was acknowledged to be unique. As we have noted, his crusty secretary of war, Edward M. Stanton, standing at Lincoln's deathbed, reportedly said, "Now he belongs to the ages." Soon people realized and publicly proclaimed that this was more true of Lincoln than of ordinary men, or ordinary presidents, or even the "great" presidents. Lincoln, dying at the end of the war he had led to preserve the Union, was a martyr to his nation. He was on his way to being thought of as the nation's redeemer. This great elevation was made possible by what scholars have called the American "political religion."

THE AMERICAN POLITICAL RELIGION

Many students of religion in the United States have noted that alongside the religious faiths that many Americans hold, reflected in their support of various denominations, there exists an equally important secular religion. This secular faith, which some call the American civil religion and others the American political religion, serves to unify the nation, which embraces many varied and sometimes contradictory religious faiths. Jews, Catholics, Protestants, and other groups find in this secular religion a tie that binds them together in patriotism without threatening their various personal or denominational faiths.

The American political religion grew out of the peculiar American experience with organized religion. Many Europeans came to America for religious reasons: to practice their faith freely and to create a society based on their religious principles. But by the time of the American Revolution there were so many competing religious groups that in the First Amendment to the new nation's Constitution the Founding Fathers forbade Congress to make any law "respecting an establishment of religion, or prohibiting the free exercise thereof." Religion was to be a matter of personal conviction and practice, and as Thomas Jefferson suggested there would be a wall of separation between church and state. Yet in those early, heady days when Americans were separating religion and politics, their leaders acknowledged that even a nation whose political system was secular needed a binding faith in a providential God to guide it through troubled waters to a safe future. Thus the American political religion was born.

This civil religion, quite naturally given the historical background of Americans, follows a format derived from Judaism and Christianity and uses symbols and language borrowed from these two interconnected faiths. For example, it identifies the American Revolution with the Hebrew exodus from Egyptian bondage: Americans escaped British bondage under the leadership of the American Moses, George Washington, its supreme general and later first president. The United States Constitution, written to create "a more perfect Union," is a document that all Americans accept as authoritative, even when they do not agree about what it means, and thus serves as the Bible, or Holy Scripture, of the republic. The American flag, under which all U.S. citizens live, which they salute, and for which so many have died, is the American civil religion's cross or Star of David. However, most Americans are probably unaware, until it is pointed out to them, that this political religion exists.

In this secular, unifying religion the president of the United States has an important role. Because of his position at the top of the government, as a single executive as opposed to a collective congress or court, because of his oath to uphold the Constitution and protect the nation from all threats, because of the ceremony of his office, the president serves as a kind of high priest or senior minister of the political religion. Before Lincoln's election some presidents had willingly and knowingly assumed this role. None of them, however, was as aware of or as comfortable with this ministerial role than Lincoln was. Although apparently not personally religious, Lincoln in the late 1850s began to use religious language in his speeches and did so consistently in his presidential addresses after his election and inauguration. His speeches were political sermons that called on the faithful to save the Union church. He was the first president completely committed to the role of high priest in the American political religion.

LINCOLN'S OWN RELIGIOUS FAITH

There is an irony in Lincoln's willingness to use religious symbols and language in his role as the nation's leader. He may well have been our least personally religious president. In his youth he doubted the claims of churches, and while he read and appreciated the Bible as great literature and would as president quote it freely, he never joined a church or made a personal profession of religious faith. He admitted that frontier preachers and their ignorant ranting repulsed him, and he often argued against the central dogmas of Christianity. When he was accused of infidelity while running for Congress in 1846, he answered in the verbally precise but philosophically evasive phrasing of a lawyer that he had never denied the "truth" of Scripture and was not an "open scoffer at Christianity." Law partner William Herndon in his Lincoln biography concluded, "Lincoln had no faith. In order to believe, he must see and feel, and thrust his hand into the place. He must taste, smell, and handle before he had faith or even belief."

Address delivered at the dedication of the
Cemetery at Gettysburg.

Four score and seven years ago our fathers
brought forth on this continent, a new nation, conceived in Liberty, and dedicated
to the proposition that all men are created equal.

Now we are engaged in a great civil war,
testing whether that nation, or any nation
so conceived and so dedicated, can long
endure. We are met on a great battle-field
of that war. We have come to dedicate a
portion of that field, as a final resting
place for those who here gave their lives,
that that nation might live. It is altogether fitting and proper that we should
do this.

But, in a larger sense, we can not dedicate— we can not consecrate— we can not
hallow— this ground. The brave men, living and dead, who struggled here, have consecrated it, far above our poor power to add

In the brief words of a speech delivered at the Gettysburg cemetery in 1863, President Lincoln renewed and in many ways refocused the nation's historic role of extending liberty to all. The speech became one of the central passages of "scripture" in the American political religion.

Herndon marshaled many witnesses to support this claim of Lincoln's agnosticism. One man, who preferred to remain anonymous, recalled from meeting Lincoln in 1838:

> Sometimes Lincoln bordered on atheism. He went far that way, and shocked me. I was then a young man, and believed what my good mother told me. . . . He would come into the clerk's office where I and some young men were writing and staying, and would bring the Bible with him; would read a chapter and argue against it. . . . Lincoln was as enthusiastic in his infidelity. As he grew older he grew more discreet; didn't talk much before strangers about his religion; but to friends, close and bosom ones, he was always open and avowed, fair and honest; to strangers, he held them off from policy.

Herndon also quoted John L. Stuart, who had been Lincoln's first law partner, as to Lincoln's attitude toward religion:

> He was an avowed and open infidel and sometimes bordered on atheism; . . . [he] went further against Christian beliefs and doctrines and principles than any man I ever heard; he shocked me. I don't remember the exact line of his argument; suppose it was against the inherent defects, so-called, of the Bible, and on grounds of reason. Lincoln always denied that Jesus was the Christ of God—denied that Jesus was the son of God as understood and maintained by the Christian Church.

Herndon understood that Americans of the 1880s and 1890s wanted to remember Lincoln as an orthodox Christian, and he almost apologized for his bluntness, but he said he felt bound by duty to tell the truth about Lincoln's personal infidelity. In one passage he wrote:

> Inasmuch as he was so often a candidate for public office Mr. Lincoln said as little about his religious opinions as possible, especially if he failed to coincide with the orthodox world. In illustration of his religious code I once heard him say that it was like that of an old man named Glenn, in Indiana, whom he heard speak at a church meeting, and who said: "When I do good I feel good, when I do bad I feel bad, and that's my religion." In 1834, while still living in New Salem and before he became a lawyer, he was surrounded by a class of people exceedingly liberal in matters of religion. Volney's "ruins" and Paine's "age of reason" passed from hand to hand, and furnished food for the evening's discussion in the tavern and village store. Lincoln read both these books and thus assimilated them into his own being. He prepared an extended essay—called by many, a book—in which he made an argument against Christianity, striving to prove that the Bible was not inspired, and therefore not God's revelation,

and that Jesus Christ was not the son of God. The manuscript containing these audacious and comprehensive propositions he intended to have published or given a wide circulation in some other way. He carried it to the store, where it was read and freely discussed. His friend and employer, Samuel Hill, was among the listeners, and, seriously questioning the propriety of a promising young man like Lincoln fathering such unpopular notions, he snatched the manuscript from his hands and thrust it into the stove. The book went up in flames, and Lincoln's political future was secure.

Yet Herndon did admit that Lincoln, though not an orthodox Christian, had a keen interest in dreams, signs, various forms of folk magic, superstitions, and particularly in fate or destiny. He described this side of Lincoln's character this way:

There was more or less superstition in his nature, and, although he may not have believed implicitly in the signs of his many dreams, he was constantly endeavoring to unravel them. His mind was readily impressed with some of the most absurd superstitions. His visit to the voodoo fortune-teller in New Orleans in 1831; his faith in the virtues of the mad-stone, when he took his son Robert to Terre Haute, Indiana, to be cured of the bite of a rabid dog; and the strange double image of himself which he told his secretary, John Hay, he saw reflected in a mirror just after his election in 1860, strongly attest his inclination to superstition. He held most firmly to the doctrine of fatalism all his life. His wife, after his death, told me what I already knew, that "his only philosophy was, what is to be will be, and no prayers of ours can reverse the decree." He always contended that he was doomed to a sad fate, and he repeatedly said to me when we were alone in our office: "I am sure I shall meet with some terrible end." In proof of his strong leaning towards fatalism he once quoted the case of Brutus and Caesar, arguing that the former was forced by laws and conditions over which he had no control to kill the latter, and *vice versa,* that the latter was specially created to be disposed of by the former. This superstitious view of life ran through his being like the thin blue vein through the whitest marble, giving the eye rest from the weariness of continued unvarying color.

Beyond this level of superstition, however, Lincoln seems to have had exactly the kind of personal convictions that, turned in the right direction, would make him the perfect minister or high priest of the American political religion. A Lincoln friend I. W. Keys told Herndon:

In my intercourse with Mr. Lincoln I learned that he believed in a Creator of all things, who had neither beginning nor end, possessing all power and wisdom, established a principle in obedience to which worlds move and are upheld, and animal and vegetable life come into existence. A reason he gave for his belief was that in view of the order and harmony of all nature which we behold, it would have been more miraculous to have come about by chance than to have been created and arranged by some great thinking power. As to the Christian theory that Christ is God or equal to the Creator, he said that it had better be taken for granted; for by the test of reason we might become infidels on that subject, for evidence of Christ's divinity came to us in a somewhat doubtful shape; but that the system of Christianity was an ingenious one at least, and perhaps was calculated to do good.

Another close Lincoln friend Jesse W. Fells told Herndon:

On the innate depravity of man, the character and office of the great Head of the Church, the atonement, the infallibility of the written revelation, the performance of miracles, the nature and design of present and future rewards and punishments (as they are popular called), and many other subjects he held opinions utterly at variance with what are usually taught in the Church. I should say that his expressed views on these and kindred topics were such as, in the estimation of most believers, would place him outside the Christian pale. Yet, to my mind, such was not the true position, since his principles and practices and the spirit of his whole life were of the very kind we universally agree to call Christian; and I think this conclusion is in no wise affected by the circumstance that he never attached himself to any religious society whatever.

His religious views were eminently practical, and are summed up, as I think, in these two propositions: the Fatherhood of God, and the brotherhood of man. He full believed in a superintending and overruling Providence that guides and controls the operations of the world, but maintained that law and order, and not their violation or suspension are the appointed means by which this Providence is exercised.

This last paragraph lays out a perfect set of principles for the American political religion: the fatherhood of God, a very general God who would please almost all Americans and offend very few; the brotherhood of man, broad enough to give unity to American society without approaching the ticklish question of salvation or doctrine, and a providence that assures the nation of God's care without being theologically specific about how or through what medium that care is provided. Lincoln the skeptic, the cynic, perhaps even the agnostic, was almost perfectly fitted with a set of general religious principles that satisfied a nation's need for a unifying, comforting, inspiring political faith in the moment of its greatest crisis.

THE FATHER, AND THE SAVIOUR OF OUR COUNTRY.

An early illustration of Lincoln's place, next to Washington, in the American political religion.

LINCOLN IN THE ROLE OF HIGH PRIEST: THE THUROW THESIS

As Lincoln neared his goal of being elected president, his speeches grew ever more religious in tone. He quoted Scripture. He spoke of God, of God's providence, of God's will. We can never know how much of this religious language reflected a late-blooming personal conviction, a theatrical or even cynical response to his growing popularity, or a self-conscious acceptance of the fact that a president must serve as high priest of the American political religion. Whatever the case, he became arguably the most successful presidential high priest ever of the American political religion. Historian Glen Thurow, in an analysis of Lincoln's presidential speeches, has masterfully demonstrated how Lincoln publicly fulfilled the religious requirements of his office. The following excerpt is from Thurow's contribution to Gabor Boritt's book *The Historian's Lincoln.*

> It must be stressed that Lincoln's speeches were political speeches, not personal confessions. Religion is present in Lincoln's speeches because of its relevance to political problems. Much of the confusion surrounding Lincoln's religion stems from the fact that commentators have tried to see whether he belonged to the religion of the churches, neglecting the possibility that his speeches were political, not religious; or were religious because they were political. In Lincoln's speeches one cannot find personal piety divorced from politics. Lincoln leads us not to religion, but to political religion. The Gettysburg Address and the Second Inaugural are the speeches of Lincoln in which religious language is most apparent and pervasive; they are also the speeches that contain or point to Lincoln's most enduring reflections on American politics.

Thurow analyzes the Gettysburg Address in detail before turning to the best example of Lincoln's religious oratory, the second inaugural. In this latter speech he is most clearly speaking as the high priest of the American religion.

> The subject of Lincoln's Second Inaugural Address, delivered as the war neared its close, is the ground on which the two sections [North and South] might be rejoined. Its intent is to point away from war toward reunion. The heart of the speech, its second and third paragraphs, is a compact piece of rhetoric. These paragraphs conclude that neither the intentions nor the prayers of the people have been fulfilled in the course of the war, and that the judgment of God must

be said to be just if the war is a punishment for the sin of slavery. The speech attempts to end the war in people's minds (even as it would soon be ended on the battlefield) by convincing them that the war is a completed action and that justice has been done. They need no longer be the warriors of justice. Charity may rule their actions.

It is in Lincoln's speculations on the meaning of the Civil War that his political religion becomes fully revealed. To see its character let us follow Lincoln's argument with some care.

In searching for the meaning of the war, Lincoln first concludes that it has not been determined by intentions or prayers. Both North and South "looked for an easier triumph, and a result less fundamental and astounding. . . . The prayers of both could not be answered; that of neither has been answered fully." A third possibility remains—that people are not the source of the meaning of the war. "The Almighty has His own purposes."

The Almighty's purposes are expressed in the words of Matthew 18:7: "Woe unto the world because of offences for it must needs be that offences come; but woe to that man by whom the offence cometh." Lincoln applies this quotation to the Civil War by asking and answering a question. The question is unexpected. It is neither "What are the purposes of God in the present situation?" nor "What is the relationship between God's purposes and ours in the present situation?" but, "Assuming God's purposes, what are we to say about His qualities?": "If we shall suppose that American Slavery is one of those offences which, in the providence of God, must needs come, but which, having continued through His appointed time, He now wills to remove, and that He gives to both North and South, this terrible war, as the woe due to those by whom the offence came, shall we discern therein any departure from those divine attributes which the believers in a living God always ascribe to Him?"

The answer has nothing to do with whether one likes the war, or whether the war is terrible. "Fondly do we hope—fervently do we pray—that this mighty scourge of war may speedily pass away. Yet, if God wills that it continue, until all the wealth piled up by the bondman's two hundred and fifty years of unrequited toil shall be sunk, and until every drop of blood drawn with the lash, shall be paid by another drawn with the sword, as was said three thousand years ago, so still it must be said 'the judgments of the Lord, are true and righteous altogether.'" Thus, in the words of Psalm 19:9 Lincoln finds the order in God that he found wanting in human intentions and prayers.

Now the character of Lincoln's argument needs to be precisely understood. Lincoln does not assert that God was the author of the Civil War, as a playwright is the author of a play. The only statements made about the relationship of the Civil War to God are conditional, and the only affirmation made concerns not the cause of the war but the justice of God's judgment under assumed conditions. Furthermore, the hypothetical conditions under which Lincoln affirms that the judgments of God could be declared just are not restricted to the actual circumstances of the war. The judgments of God would be just if the war continued until all the bondman's wealth should be destroyed and the blood drawn with the lash paid for with the sword.

In understanding what Lincoln does claim to know about the purposes of God, we have the testimony of Lincoln upon the precise point in a letter to Thurlow Weed[1] written shortly after the inaugural. Lincoln wrote that he expected the Second Inaugural to wear as well as and perhaps better than anything he had written. However, it was not immediately popular: "Men are not flattered by being shown that there has been a difference of purpose between the Almighty and them. To deny it, however, in this case, is to deny that there is a God governing the world. It is a truth which I thought needed to be told; and as whatever of humiliation there is in it, falls most directly on myself, I thought others might afford for me to tell it."

Lincoln perceives a gulf between human purposes and God's and comes to this perception by seeing the imperfection of human purposes. What becomes clear is not the content of God's purposes, but that they differ from ours. This central truth is placed in the inaugural immediately following Lincoln's discussion of prayer, and reveals the importance of prayer. We may note that although prayer may be rational in content, it is folly to believe that God can be given directions even through our prayers. To ask God for something assumes that human reason may govern the world. But "the Almighty has His own Purposes." Prayer shares the limits of human reason, but does not confess them. Because Lincoln sees the limits of our purposes and prayers, he is able to see that they are not God's.

One can see the kinship of the Second Inaugural to that skepticism for which Lincoln was noted among his friends. The faith that regards providence as essentially unknowable and the skepticism of all providence agree that the pattern of future events cannot be known and hence that our capacity to manage the future is limited. . . .

The Second Inaugural suggests that people must participate in God's order by acknowledging the justice of God. But we may note that they cannot transcend the nation in this sense unassisted. They need someone who will point out to them what God's judgment is. All too often people will think that God's judgment is the same as the nation's judgment, or, conversely, they will substitute their private judgment for the nation's judgment. They do not see by themselves that "the Almighty has His own purposes." The need of democratic citizens to transcend the nation can be fulfilled only if they have a guide who stands between God and themselves.

---

[1] Weed, editor of the *Albany Evening Journal,* was a Republican Party chieftain in New York state.

LINCOLN IN THE ROLE OF REDEEMER: THE BELLAH THESIS

Lincoln was indeed the consummate high priest of America's secular religion. But because he died when and how he did—and was perceived as a martyr to the cause of national union, a lamb sacrificed to end the war, reconcile a divided people, and heal the nation's wounds—he began in death to play an even higher role. He became the political religious redeemer.

Robert Bellah, a historian of religion in America, was the first scholar to explain clearly the highest of all Lincoln roles. He wrote about this role, using the term "civil religion," in the scholarly magazine *Daedalus* in 1967. In the following excerpt from that seminal article, after tracing the emergence of the American civil religion from the "Exodus" from British bondage to the establishment of the national "church" on the "scriptural" Declaration of Independence and United States Constitution, Bellah comes to the Civil War and Lincoln.

> Until the Civil War, the American civil religion focused above all on the event of the Revolution, which was seen as the final act of the Exodus from the old lands across the waters. The Declaration of Independence and the Constitution were the sacred scriptures and Washington the divinely appointed Moses who led his people out of the hands of tyranny. The Civil War, which Sidney Mead[2] calls "the center of American history," was the second great event that involved the national self-understanding so deeply as to require expression in the civil religion. In 1835, de Tocqueville[3] wrote that the American republic had never really been tried, that victory in the Revolutionary War was more the result of British preoccupation elsewhere and the presence of a powerful ally than of any great military success of the Americans. But in 1861 the time of testing had indeed come. Not only did the Civil War have the tragic intensity of fratricidal strife, but it was one of the bloodiest wars of the nineteenth century; the loss of life was far greater than any previously suffered by Americans. . . .

> With the Civil War, a new theme of death, sacrifice, and rebirth enters the civil religion. It is symbolized in the life and death of Lincoln. Nowhere is it stated more vividly than in the Gettysburg Address, itself part of the Lincolnian "New Testament" among the civil scriptures.

---

[2] Mead is the author of many studies of religion in the American republic, including *The Old Religion in the Brave New World.*

[3] Alexis de Tocqueville, a Frenchman who visited America in the 1830s, wrote *Democracy in America.*

Robert Lowell[4] has recently pointed out the "insistent use of birth images" in this speech explicitly devoted to "these honored dead": "brought forth," "conceived," "created," "a new birth of freedom." He goes on to say:

> The Gettysburg Address is a symbolic and sacramental act. Its verbal quality is resonance combined with a logical, matter of fact, prosaic brevity. In his words, Lincoln symbolically died, just as the Union soldiers really died—and as he himself was soon really to die. By his words, he gave the field of battle a symbolic significance that it had lacked. For us and our country, he left Jefferson's ideals of freedom and equality joined to the Christian sacrificial act of death and rebirth. I believe this is a meaning that goes beyond sect or religion and beyond peace and war, and is now part of our lives as a challenge, obstacle and hope.

Lowell is certainly right in pointing out the Christian quality of the symbolism here, but he is also right in quickly disavowing any sectarian implication. The earlier symbolism of the civil religion had been Hebraic without being in any specific sense Jewish. The Gettysburg symbolism (". . those who here gave their lives, that that nation might live") is Christian without being anything to do with the Christian church.

The symbolic equation of Lincoln with Jesus was made relatively early. [William] Herndon, who had been Lincoln's law partner, wrote:

> For fifty years God rolled Abraham Lincoln through his fiery furnace. He did it to try Abraham and to purify him for his purposes. This made Mr. Lincoln humble, tender, forbearing, sympathetic to suffering, kind, sensitive, tolerant; broadening, deepening and widening his whole nature; making him the noblest and loveliest character since Jesus Christ. . . . I believe that Lincoln was God's chosen one.

With the Christian archetype in the background, Lincoln, "our martyred president," was linked to the war dead, those who ". . . gave the last full measure of devotion." The theme of sacrifice was indelibly written into the civil religion.

Abraham Lincoln himself was indelibly written into the American political religion as the agent of redemption. This happened quickly, the first words of his chapter in the religious saga being written immediately after his death, the rest fleshed out in the months and years that followed. By the beginning of the twentieth century the story had been told, and only subtle nuances would be added in the constant retelling thereafter.

---

[4] Lowell, a twentieth-century poet, wrote *Life Studies for the Union Dead.*

CREATORS OF "LINCOLN THE REDEEMER" IMAGE

The Poets

Lincoln was established as the redeemer in the American political religion by poets and orators, and the process is easy to trace in their surviving poems and speeches. They grieved along with the American public and spoke of Lincoln's unique place in American history and in their hearts. American poets at the time of Lincoln's death were unusually adept at capturing the spirit of their time. Their responses to the assassination, written in April 1865, amid the outpouring of public grief that followed it, were the first contributions to a lengthy body of words that cumulatively led to Lincoln's sanctification as a national hero.

WALT WHITMAN

One of the first poets to express his grief was Walt Whitman, author of *Leaves of Grass.* Although Whitman would later express some embarrassment at the effusive language he used in "O Captain! My Captain!" the poem affirmed Lincoln's role as national leader during the republic's darkest hours and as the very prototype of what an American president should be.

> O Captain! my Captain! our fearful trip is done,
> The ship has weathered every rack, the prize we sought is won,
> The port is near, the bells I hear, the people all exulting,
> While follow eyes the steady keel, the vessel grim and daring;
> > But O heart! heart! heart!
> > > O the bleeding drops of red,
> > > > Where on the deck my Captain lies,
> > > > > Fallen cold and dead.
>
> O Captain! my Captain! rise up and hear the bells;
> Rise up—for you the flag is flung—for you the bugle trills,
> For you bouquets and ribbon'd wreaths—for you the shores
> a-crowding,
> For you they call, the swaying mass, their eager faces turning;
> > Here Captain! dear father!
> > > The arm beneath your head!
> > > > It is some dream that on the deck,
> > > > > You've fallen cold and dead.

My Captain does not answer, his lips are pale and still,
My father does not feel my arm, he has no pulse nor will,
The ship is anchor'd safe and sound, its voyage closed and done,
From fearful trip the victor ship comes in with object won;
    Exult O shores, and ring O bells!
      But I with mournful tread,
        Walk the deck my Captain lies,
          Fallen cold and dead.

WILLIAM CULLEN BRYANT

In the same month in which Whitman described Lincoln as the nation's fallen captain, the aging, much revered William Cullen Bryant penned his poem "The Death of Lincoln." This time Lincoln was identified as the liberator, the man who freed slaves, who perished for the right. Bryant, whose masterpiece was "Thanatopsis," a meditation on death, was well qualified to interpret the end of Lincoln's life on earth. This poem was read, along with Lincoln's Second Inaugural Address, at memorial services when his body passed through New York City.

Oh, slow to smite and swift to spare
    Gentle and merciful and just!
Who, in the fear of God, didst bear
    The sword of power, a nation's trust!

In sorrow by thy bier we stand,
    Amid the awe that hushes all,
And speak the anguish of a land
    That shook with horror at thy fall.

Thy task is done; the bond are free:
    We bear thee to an honored grave,
Whose proudest monument shall be
    The broken fetters of the slave.

Pure was thy life; its bloody close
    Hath placed thee with the sons of light,
Among the noble host of those
    Who perished in the cause of Right.

Lincoln was already, in the nation's mind, and in the gifted language of Bryant, among the "sons of light" because he "perished in the cause of Right."

HERMAN MELVILLE

The third of the triumvirate of poets to eulogize Lincoln and add to his emerging image was Herman Melville, author of *Moby Dick*. In his poem "The Martyr," also penned in April 1865, he gave the assassination a decidedly theological interpretation. Lincoln, sent to bring forgiveness, to do God's work on earth, had died on Good Friday. His blood was shed for the nation, and those who killed him should beware.

> Good Friday was the day
>   Of the prodigy and crime,
> When they killed him in his pity,
>   When they killed him in his prime
> Of clemency and calm—
>   When with yearning he was filled
>   To redeem the evil-willed,
> And, though conqueror, be kind;
>   But they killed him in his kindness,
>   In their madness and their blindness,
> And they killed him from behind.
>
> There is sobbing of the strong,
>   And a pall upon the land
> But the People in their weeping
> ·   Bare the iron hand:
> Beware the People weeping
>   When they bare the iron hand.
>
> He lieth in his blood—
>   The father in his face;
> They have killed him, the Forgiver—
>   The Avenger takes his place,
> The Avenger wisely stern,
>   Who in righteousness shall do
>   What the heavens call him to,
> And the parricides remand;
>   For they killed him in his kindness,
>   In their madness and their blindness,
> And his blood is on their hand.
>
> There is sobbing of the strong,
>   And a pall upon the land;
> But the People in their weeping
>   Bare the iron hand:
> Beware the People weeping
>   When they bare the iron hand.

EDMUND STEDMAN

Melville, though the most prominent, was not the first poet to interpret Lincoln's death theologically. On the Easter Sunday when Lincoln lay in his casket, Edmund Stedman's eulogy was published in the *New York Tribune*. Stedman, an early abolitionist, had served in the Army of the Potomac. In his poem he went so far as to place the words of the crucified, dying Jesus into the martyred president's mouth.

> "Forgive them, for they know not what they do!"
>   He said, and so went shriven to his fate,—
> Unknowing went, that generous heart and true.
>   Even while he spoke the slayer lay in wait,
> And when the morning opened Heaven's gate
>   There passed the whitest soul a nation knew.
> Henceforth all thoughts of pardon are too late;
>   They, in whose cause that arm its weapon drew,
> Have murdered Mercy. Now alone shall stand
>   Blind Justice, with the sword unsheathed she wore.
> Hark, from the eastern to the western strand,
>   The swelling thunder of the people's roar:
> What words they murmur,—Fetter not her hand!
>   So let it smite, such deeds shall be no more!

EDWIN MARKHAM

The image of Lincoln as the great leader, liberator of the oppressed, and martyr for the cause of freedom and union grew sharper with time, as his pale successors struggled to solve problems that might well have stumped him as well. And the image grew ever more religious. In 1909, the year of Lincoln's one-hundredth birthday, the poet Edwin Markham, in his "Young Lincoln," wrote of the future captain of state being laid as an infant in the hollow of a log, humblest of cradles except for "that other one—the manger in the stall at Bethlehem." Hidden in the west, "God shaped his man," Markham wrote, his only defect being his willingness "to bend the law to let his mercy out." Treason struck him down, but

> Lincoln is not dead. He lives
> In all that pities and forgives.
> He has arisen and sheds a fire
> That makes America aspire.

Even now as, when in life, he led,
He leads us onward from the dead;
Yes, over the whole wide world he bends
To make the world a world of friends.

JAMES WHITCOMB RILEY

It was the Hoosier poet James Whitcomb Riley who wrote the lines that confirmed Lincoln's place in the popular imagination as the Christ of the American passion play. The elements were all there. Lincoln the martyr, the lamb sacrificed for America's redemption, was shot on Good Friday. Five days earlier, on Palm Sunday, he had returned to the nation's capitol in triumph from a battlefield in Virginia, on the very day Lee had surrendered to Grant. All symbols were aligned.

Riley, known as the "poet of democracy," remembered at age eleven seeing his father return from Chicago to tell how he had helped nominate Lincoln for president, and he remembered how at age sixteen he had mourned the president's death. Past fifty when he wrote these words, he proclaimed Lincoln the man of sorrows who died to save his nation's soul.

A peaceful life;—just toil and rest—
　　All his desire;—
To read the books he liked the best
　　Beside the cabin fire—
God's word and man's;—to peer sometimes
　　Above the page, in smoldering gleams,
And catch, like far heroic rhymes,
　　The on-march of his dreams.

A peaceful life;—to hear the low
　　Of pastured herds,
Of woodman's ax that, blow on blow,
　　Fell sweet as rhythmic words.
And yet there stirred within his breast
　　A fateful pulse that, like a roll
Of drums, made high above his rest
　　A tumult in his soul.

A peaceful life! . . . They haled him even
　　As One was haled
Whose open palms were nailed toward Heaven
　　When prayers nor aught availed.

And, lo, he paid the selfsame price
　To lull a nation's awful strife
And will us, through the sacrifice
　Of self, his peaceful life.

VACHEL LINDSAY

In 1909 Vachel Lindsay gave Riley's abstract image of Lincoln as
Christ a concrete touch. He portrayed a resurrected Lincoln still
walking among his people, watching over the nation he loved. Lindsay grew up near Lincoln's Illinois home and knew Springfield well.
Admiration for Lincoln came late to Lindsay, for his family had opposed emancipation of the slaves, but he became one of the Great
Emancipator's most ardent hymnists. In "Abraham Lincoln Walks at
Midnight" he portrayed a risen leader, brooding over his people,
bearing their burdens, suffering still for their shortcomings.

It is portentous, and a thing of state
That here at midnight, in our little town
A mourning figure walks, and will not rest,
Near the old court-house pacing up and down,

Or by his homestead, or its shadowed yards
He lingers where his children used to play,
Or through the market, on the well-worn stones
He stalks until the dawn-stars burn away.

A bronzed, lank man! His suit of ancient black,
A famous high-top hat and plain worn shawl
Make him the quaint great figure that men love,
The prairie-lawyer, master of us all.

He cannot sleep upon his hillside now.
He is among us:—as in times before!
And we who toss and lie awake for long,
Breathe deep, and start, to see him pass the door.

His head is bowed. He thinks of men and kings.
Yea, when the sick world cries, how can he sleep?
Too many peasants fight, they know not why;
Too many homesteads in black terror weep.

The sins of all the war-lords burn his heart.
He sees the dreadnaughts scouring every main.
He carries on his shawl-wrapped shoulders now
The bitterness, the folly and the pain.

He cannot rest until a spirit-dawn
Shall come;—the shining hope of Europe free:
A league of sober folk, the workers' earth,
Bringing long peace to Cornland, Alp and Sea.

It breaks his heart that kings must murder still,
That all his hours of travail here for men
Seem yet in vain. And who will bring white peace
That he may sleep upon his hill again?

The poets reached every religious group in America with their story of Lincoln, the Christ-like redeemer of the American civil religion. In 1910 Rabbi Joseph Silverman of Temple Emmanuel in New York City proclaimed, "There is no need to preach the precepts of the Bible when we have such a real Messiah, who lived in the flesh and never pretended to be more than a man."

The Orators

If the poets caught the mood of the American people and helped establish the myth of Lincoln as heroic leader, liberator, and savior, the orators spread these images to the masses, and continue to do so. They have kept alive his memory for each new generation.

RALPH WALDO EMERSON

On April 19, 1865, only four days after Lincoln's death, Ralph Waldo Emerson addressed the congregation of the Unitarian Church in Concord, Massachusetts. As one of the leading exponents of the philosophy known as transcendentalism, Emerson was an eloquent writer and public orator. His speech honoring the slain leader of the Union helped to set the stage for a steady stream of tributes to Lincoln that would last for more than a century.

> We meet under the gloom of a calamity which darkens down over the minds of good men in all civil society, as the fearful tidings travel over sea, from country to country, like the shadow of an uncalculated eclipse over the planet. Old as history is, and manifold as are its tragedies, I doubt if any death has caused so much pain to mankind as this has caused, or will cause, on its announcement; and this, not so much because nations are by modern arts brought so closely together, as because of the mysterious hopes and fears which, in the present day, are connected with the name and institutions of America.

In this country, on Saturday, every one was struck dumb, and saw at first only deep below deep, as he meditated on the ghastly blow. And perhaps, at this hour, when the coffin which contains the dust of the President sets forward on its long march through mourning states, on its way to its home in Illinois, we might well be silent, and suffer the awful voices of the time to thunder to us. Yes, but that first despair was brief: the man was not so to be mourned. He was the most active and hopeful of men; and his work had not perished: but acclamations of praise for the task he had accomplished burst out into a song of triumph, which even tears for his death cannot keep down.

The President stood before us as a man of the people. He was thoroughly American, had never crossed the sea, had never been spoiled by English insularity or French dissipation; a quite native, aboriginal man, as an acorn from the oak; no aping of foreigners, no frivolous accomplishments, Kentuckian born, working on a farm, a flatboatman, a captain in the Black Hawk War, a country lawyer, a representative in the rural legislature of Illinois;—on such modest foundations the broad structure of his fame was laid. How slowly, and yet by happily prepared steps, he came to his place. All of us remember—it is only a history of five or six years—the surprise and the disappointment of the country at his first nomination by the convention in Chicago. Mr. Seward, then in the culmination of his good fame, was the favorite of the Eastern States. And when the new and comparatively unknown name of Lincoln was announced (notwithstanding the report of the acclamations of that convention), we heard the result coldly and sadly. It seemed too rash, on a purely local reputation, to build so grave a trust in such anxious times; and men naturally talked of the chances in politics as incalculable. But it turned out not to be chance. The profound good opinion which the people of Illinois and of the West had conceived of him, and which they had imparted to their colleagues, that they also might justify themselves to their constituents at home, was not rash, though they did not begin to know the riches of his worth. . . .

His occupying the chair of state was a triumph of the good sense of mankind, and of the public conscience. This middle-class country had got a middle-class president, at last. Yes, in manners and sympathies, but not in powers, for his powers were superior. This man grew according to the need. His mind mastered the problem of the day; and as the problem grew, so did his comprehension of it. Rarely was man so fitted to the event. In the midst of fears and jealousies, in the Babel of counsels and parties, this man wrought incessantly with all his might and all his honesty, laboring to find what the people wanted, and how to obtain that. It cannot be said there is any exaggeration of his worth. If ever a man was fairly tested, he was. There was no lack of resistance, nor of slander, nor of ridicule. The times have allowed no state secrets; the nation has been in such ferment, such multitudes had to be trusted, that no secret could be kept. Every door was ajar, and we know all that befell.

Then, what an occasion was the whirlwind of the war. Here was place for no holiday magistrate, no fair-weather sailor; the new pilot was hurried to the helm in a tornado. In four years—four years of battle-days,—his endurance, his fertility of resources, his magnanimity, were sorely tried and never found wanting. There, by his courage, his justice, his even temper, his fertile counsel, his humanity, he stood a heroic figure in the centre of a heroic epoch. He is the true history of the American people in his time. Step by step he walked before them; slow with their slowness, quickening his march by theirs, the true representative of this continent; an entirely public man; father of his country, the pulse of twenty millions throbbing in his heart, the thought of their minds articulated by his tongue. . . .

The ancients believed in a serene and beautiful Genius which ruled in the affairs of nations; which, with a slow and stern justice, carried forward the fortunes of certain chosen houses, weeding out single offenders or offending families, and securing at last the firm prosperity of the favorites of Heaven. It was too narrow a view of the Eternal Nemesis. There is a serene Providence which rules the fate of nations, which makes little account of time, little of one generation or race, makes no account of disasters, conquers alike by what is called defeat or by what is called victory, thrusts aside enemy and obstruction, crushes everything immoral as inhuman, and obtains the ultimate triumph of the best race by the sacrifice of everything which resists the moral laws of the world. It makes its own instruments, creates the man for the time, trains him in poverty, inspires his genius, and arms him for his task. It has given every race its own talent, and ordains that only that race which combines perfectly with the virtues of all shall endure.

WOODROW WILSON

Through the rest of the nineteenth century, Lincoln was the subject of both political and religious oratory. His Republican Party elected all but one president from 1860 to 1912, and all of these men looked back to Lincoln as their example. Both political leaders and religious leaders used his image to confirm and buttress their causes. He came to embody each succeeding generation's ideals, hopes, and dreams. By 1912, when Democrat Woodrow Wilson was elected in a year in which Republicans split their votes between two candidates, former President Theodore Roosevelt and sitting President William Howard Taft, Lincoln had become the inspiration of both parties. A leader of the Progressive movement, Wilson saw in Lincoln what he himself wanted to be: a crusader against monopolies and for struggling entrepreneurs. The following speech was delivered on September 4, 1916, when Wilson went to Kentucky to dedicate the Lincoln birthplace as a national monument. Events were conspiring to bring the United States into World War I, and Wilson seemed anxious to identify himself with Lincoln, who had also led an unpopular but righteous war.

No more significant memorial could have been presented to the nation than this. It expresses so much of what is singular and noteworthy in the history of the country; it suggests so many of the things that we prize most highly in our life and in our system of government. How eloquent this little house within this shrine is of the vigor of democracy! There is nowhere in the land any home so remote, so humble, that it may not contain the power of mind and heart and conscience to which nations yield and history submits its processes. Nature pays no tribute to aristocracy, subscribes to no creed of caste, renders fealty to no monarch or master of any name or kind. Genius is no snob. It does not run after titles or seek by preference the high circles of society. It affects humble company as well as great. It pays no special tribute to universities or learned societies or conventional standards of greatness, but serenely chooses its own comrades, its own haunts, its own cradle even, and its own life of adventure and of training. Here is proof of it. This little hut was the cradle of one of the great sons of men, a man of singular, delightful, vital genius who presently emerged upon the great stage of the nation's history, gaunt, shy, ungainly, but dominant and majestic, a natural ruler of men, himself inevitably the central figure of the great plot. No man can explain this, but every man can see how it demonstrates the vigor of democracy, where every door is open, in every hamlet and countryside, in city and wilderness alike, for the ruler to emerge when he will and claim his leadership in the free life. Such are the authentic proofs of the validity and vitality of democracy.

Here, no less, hides the mystery of democracy. Who shall guess this secret of nature and providence and a free polity? Whatever the vigor and vitality of the stock from which he sprang, its mere vigor and soundness do not explain where this man got his great heart that seemed to comprehend all mankind in its catholic and benignant sympathy, the mind that sat enthroned behind those brooding, melancholy eyes, whose vision swept many an horizon which those about him dreamed not of,—that mind that comprehended what it had never seen, and understood the language of affairs with the ready ease of one to the manner born,—or that nature which seemed in its varied richness to be the familiar of men of every way of life. This is the sacred mystery of democracy, that its richest fruits spring up out of soils which no man has prepared and in circumstances amidst which they are the least expected. This is a place alike of mystery and of reassurance. . . .

Here Lincoln had his beginnings. Here the end and consummation of that great life seem remote and a bit incredible. And yet there was no break anywhere between beginning and end, no lack of natural sequence anywhere. Nothing really incredible happened. Lincoln was unaffectedly as much at home in the White House as he was here. Do you share with me the feeling, I wonder, that he was permanently at home nowhere? It seems to me that in the case of a man,—I would rather say of a spirit,—like Lincoln the question where he was is of little significance, that it is always what he was that really arrests our thought and takes hold of our imagination. It is the spirit always that is sovereign. Lincoln, like the rest of us, was put through the discipline of the world,—a very rough and exacting discipline for him, an indispensable discipline for every man who would know what he is about in the midst of the world's affairs; but his spirit got only its schooling there. It did not derive its character or its vision from the experiences which brought it to its full revelation. The test of every American must always be, not where he is, but what he is. That, also, is of the essence of democracy, and is the moral of which this place is most gravely expressive. . . .

I have read many biographies of Lincoln; I have sought out with the greatest interest the many intimate stories that are told of him, the narratives of nearby friends, the sketches at close quarters, in which those who had the privilege of being associated with him have tried to depict for us the very man himself "in his habit as he lived"; but I have nowhere found a real intimate of Lincoln's. I nowhere get the impression in any narrative or reminiscence that the writer had in fact penetrated to the heart of his mystery, or that any man could penetrate to the heart of it. That brooding spirit had no real familiars. I get the impression that it never spoke out in complete self-revelation, and that it could not reveal itself completely to anyone. It was a very lonely spirit that looked out from underneath those shaggy brows and comprehended men without fully communing with them, as if, in spite of all its genial efforts at comradeship, it dwelt apart, saw its visions of duty where no man looked on. There is a very holy and very terrible isolation for the conscience of every man who seeks to read the destiny in affairs for others as well as for himself, for a nation as well as for individuals. That privacy no man can intrude upon. That lonely search of the spirit for the right perhaps no man can assist. This strange child of the cabin kept company with invisible things, was born into no intimacy but that of its own silently assembling and deploying thoughts.

I have come here today, not to utter a eulogy on Lincoln; he stands in need of none, but to endeavor to interpret the meaning of this gift to the nation of the place of his birth and origin. Is not this an altar upon which we may forever keep alive the vestal fire of democracy as upon a shrine at which some of the deepest and most sacred hopes of mankind may from age to age be rekindled? For these hopes must con[s]tantly be rekindled, and only those who live can rekindle them. The only stuff that can retain the life-giving heat is the stuff of living hearts. And the hopes of mankind cannot be kept alive by words merely, by constitutions and doctrines of right and codes of liberty. The object of democracy is to transmute these into the life and action of society, the self-denial and self-sacrifice of heroic men and women willing to make their lives an embodiment of right and service and enlightened purpose. The commands of democracy are as imperative as its privileges and opportunities are wide and generous. Its compulsion is upon us. It will be great and lift a great light for the guidance of the nations only if we are great and carry that light high for the guidance of our own feet. We are not worthy to stand here unless we ourselves be in deed and in truth real democrats and servants of mankind, ready to give our very lives for the freedom and justice and spiritual exaltation of the great nation which shelters and nurtures us.

While Wilson's message was on its surface political and did not call Lincoln the redeemer, it spoke forcibly of the religious nature of American democracy (a form of religion), the role of Lincoln as its leader (its Christ-figure), and even of the sacred place of his birth (the cabin as a manger). The hut before which Wilson spoke was to him the cradle of one of the great sons of men, a place that reminded him of the sacred mystery of democracy: how greatness springs from places least appropriate to it. Lincoln is that lonely, mysterious man whose brooding spirit inspires us, and our duty is to nourish the "vestal fire" that burns in the "shrine" where Lincoln was born. Wilson's father, it might be remembered, was a Presbyterian minister.

MARIO CUOMO

An oration delivered by another Democrat, New York Governor Mario Cuomo, in Springfield on February 12, 1986, stands as one of the greatest modern tributes to Lincoln. As in Wilson's speech, Lincoln becomes what the speaker wants him to be, the exemplar of the best of American ideals. Cuomo is the son of Italian immigrants. His words reflect the great respect most newer Americans hold for the president who, through the Emancipation Proclamation, forwarded the cause of liberty not only in the United States but throughout the world. Once more we see how Lincoln, as a redeemer must, embodies the hopes, aspirations, and ideals of each succeeding generation and each new immigrant group.

Had Lincoln not existed, or had he been less than he was and the battle to keep the nation together had been lost, it would have meant the end of the American experiment. Secession would have bred secession, reducing us into smaller and smaller fragments until finally we were just the broken pieces of the dream.

Lincoln saved us from that. But winning the great war for unity did not preserve us from the need to fight further battles in the struggle to balance our diversity with our harmony, to keep the pieces of the mosaic intact, even while making room for new pieces. That work is today, as it was in 1863, still an unfinished work . . . still a cause that requires "a full measure of devotion."

For more than 100 years, the fight to include has continued:

—in the struggle to free working people from the oppression of a ruthless economic system that saw women and children worked to death and men born to poverty, live in poverty, and die in poverty—in spite of working all the time.

—in the continuing fight for civil rights, making Lincoln's promise real.

—in the effort to keep the farmer alive.

—in the ongoing resistance to preserve religious freedom from the arrogance of the Know-Nothing and the zealotry of those who would make their religion the state's religion.

—in the crusade to make women equal, legally and practically.

Many battles have been won. The embrace of our unity has been gradually but inexorably expanded. But Lincoln's work is not yet done.

A century after Lincoln preached his answer of equality and mutual respect, some discrimination—of class or race or sex or ethnicity—as a bar to full participation in America still remains. Unpleasant reminders of less enlightened times linger. Sometimes they are heard in whispers. At other times they are loud enough to capture the attention of the American people.

I have had my own encounter with this question and I have spoken of it. Like millions of others, I am privileged to be a first generation American. My mother and father came to this country more than sixty years ago with nothing but their hopes, without education, skills, or wealth. Through the opportunity given them here to lift themselves through hard work, they were able to raise a family. My mother has lived to see her youngest child become chief executive of one of the greatest states in the greatest nation in the only world we know.

Like millions of other children of immigrants, I know the strength that immigrants can bring. I know the richness of a society that allows us a whole new culture without requiring us to surrender the one our parents were born to. I know the miraculous power of this place that helps people rise up from poverty to security, and even affluence, in the course of a single lifetime. With generations of other children of the immigrants, I know about equality and opportunity and unity, in a special way.

And I know how, from time to time, all this beauty can be challenged by the misguided children of the Know-Nothings, by the short-sighted and the unkind, by contempt that masks itself as humor, by all the casual or conscious bigotry that must keep the American people vigilant.

We heard such voices again recently saying things like, Italians are not politically popular. Catholics will have a problem. He has an ethnic problem. An ethnic problem. We hear the word again, "Wop."

"We oftentimes refer to people of Italian descent as 'Wops,'" said one public figure, unabashedly. . . .

No one knew better than Lincoln our sturdiness, the ability of most of us to make it on our own given the chance. But at the same time, no one knew better the idea of family, the idea that unless we helped one another, there were some who would never make it.

One person climbs the ladder of personal ambition, reaches his dream, and then turns and pulls the ladder up. Another reaches the place he has sought, turns, and reaches down for the person behind him. With Lincoln, it was that process of turning and reaching down, that commitment to keep lifting people up the ladder, which defined the American character, stamping us forever with a mission that reached even beyond our borders to embrace the world.

Lincoln's belief in America, in the American people, was broader, deeper, more daring than any other person's of his age—and, perhaps, ours, too. And this is the near-unbelievable greatness of the man, that with that belief, he not only led us, he created us.

His personal mythology became our national mythology. It is as if Homer not only chronicled the siege of Troy, but conducted the siege as well. As if Shakespeare set his playwrighting aside to lead the English against the Armada. Because Lincoln embodied his age in his actions and in his words:

—words, even and measured, hurrying across three decades, calling us to our destiny;

—words he prayed, and troubled over, more than a million words in his speeches and writings;

—words that chronicled the search for his own identity as he searched for a nation's identity;

—words that were, by turns, as chilling as the night sky and as assuring as home;

—words his reason sharpened into steel, and his heart softened into an embrace;

—words filled with all the longings of his soul and of his century;

—words wrung from his private struggle, spun to capture the struggle of a nation;

—words out of his own pain to heal that struggle;

—words of retribution, but never of revenge;

—words that judged, but never condemned;

—words that pleaded, cajoled for the one belief—that the promise must be kept—that the dream must endure and grow, until it embraces everyone;

—words ringing down into the present;

—all the hope and the pain of that epic caught, somehow, by his cadences: the tearing away, the binding together, the leaving behind, the reaching beyond. . . .

In Lincoln's time, one of every seven Americans was a slave. Today, for all our affluence and might, despite what every day is described as our continuing economic recovery, nearly one in every seven Americans lives in poverty, not in chains—because Lincoln saved us from that—but trapped in a cycle of despair that is its own enslavement.

Today, while so many of us do so well, one of every two minority children is born poor, many of them to be oppressed for a lifetime by inadequate education and the suffocating influence of broken families and social disorientation. Our identity as a people is hostage to the grim facts of more than 33 million Americans for whom equality and opportunity is not yet an attainable reality, but only an illusion.

Some people look at these statistics and the suffering people behind them, and deny them, pretending instead we are all one great "shining city on a hill." Lincoln told us for a lifetime—and for all time to come—that there can be no shining city when one in seven of us is denied the promise of the declaration. He tells us today that we are justly proud of all that we have accomplished, but that for all our progress, for all our achievement, for all that so properly makes us proud, we have no right to rest, content; nor justification for turning from the effort, out of fear or lack of confidence.

We have met greater challenges with fewer resources. We have faced greater perils with fewer friends. It would be a desecration of our belief and an act of ingratitude for the good fortune we have had to end the struggle for inclusion because it is over for some of us.

So, this evening, we come to pay you our respects, Mr. Lincoln, not just by recalling your words and revering your memory, which we do humbly and with great pleasure.

This evening, we offer you more, Mr. President—we offer you what you have asked us for, a continuing commitment to live your truth, to go forward painful step by painful step, enlarging the greatness of this nation with patient confidence in the ultimate justice of the people.

Because, as you have told us, Mr. President, there is no better or equal hope in the world.

SUMMARY: LINCOLN AND THE FUTURE

Lincoln was born in a nation already developing what is called the American political religion. Although he was himself a skeptic, perhaps an agnostic, he rescued the fractured Union from self-destruction during the Civil War by playing the presidential role of high priest more effectively than any previous president. Then, because he held center stage at the crucial moment in American history, and especially because of his untimely and violent death, he assumed a role more exalted than that of any other president before or since. The American political religion, based on the Judeo-Christian tradition, already had in George Washington a Moses; it awaited a redeemer which it found in the person of Abraham Lincoln.

The American poets who conferred this identity on Lincoln both reflected the public mood and gave a clear voice to it. The American orators who have continued the praise worthy of a redeemer have demonstrated the way Lincoln embodies the dreams and ideals of every successive American generation and immigrant group.

As to the future, there is no reason to think that Lincoln's image will change or cease to exert its influence. Future presidents will be successful high priests and will fill other roles in the American political religion, but Lincoln will likely always be its redeemer. In that role he will continue to be a creator of the American mind.

QUESTIONS FOR RESPONSIVE ESSAYS

1. Describe what scholars call the American political (or civil) religion. What is Lincoln's role in it and why? Why has this religion and Lincoln's role in it never led traditionally religious people to charge blasphemy? How and why does this religion coexist peacefully with traditional denominational faiths?

2. Describe Lincoln's personal religious faith. Why did his friends and political allies advise him to keep it quiet? How did it fit neatly into his role as high priest of the American political religion? How did Lincoln adopt traditional religious language and concepts for effective use as president?

3. Discuss how the poets you have read contributed to the myth of Lincoln the redeemer. What language and symbols did they use to make their case? Why were the American people so ready and willing to agree with this image and adopt it as their own? Why do poems about Lincoln still find acceptance today?

4. Discuss Ralph Waldo Emerson's eulogy to Lincoln, the fallen leader. What themes did he use to describe Lincoln's achievement, and to what extent did they find a home in the American mind? What patterns of interpretation did he establish for orators to come, including Woodrow Wilson and Mario Cuomo? What contributions did the orators make to Lincoln's role as redeemer in the American political religion?

5. How has Lincoln been used, by poets and orators alike, to represent and confirm what each generation since his time has considered its best ideals? To what extent is the Lincoln celebrated by each new generation the real man, and to what extent is he a creation of wishful thinking? How can wishful thinking be helpful and how can it be harmful to a nation?

SUGGESTED TOPICS FOR PAPERS ON LINCOLN

1. *Abraham Lincoln: Citizen and President.* How did Lincoln's early life, his family life, and his career before 1860 prepare him to be the kind of president he became? What personal qualities enabled him to use both adversities and opportunities to the greatest advantage?

2. *Abraham Lincoln as the Great Emancipator.* Trace Lincoln's personal and public development from his early attitude toward slavery to his actions as president. How do you account for his caution and hesitancy, and what do his ideas about colonization say about his racial feelings? How might his personal sense of bondage as a young man have led eventually to the Emancipation Proclamation? How did Lincoln's role as emancipator lead to his role as redeemer in the American political religion?

3. *Abraham Lincoln and the American Political Religion.* Explain the nature and function of civil religion in American life and public affairs. In what ways were Americans awaiting a Lincoln? How did Lincoln consciously and unconsciously fulfill the role of redeemer? Could anyone else have fulfilled this role? What is the status of the American political religion today? Will Lincoln always be an indispensable figure in it?

4. *Abraham Lincoln: The Man and the Myth.* Show how an aura of myth enveloped Lincoln during his life and especially after his death. Why is the Lincoln myth so much stronger than that of other presidents? How possible is it to separate the man from the myth? How important is it to do so?

5. *Abraham Lincoln and Psycho-Historians.* What do historians who analyze Lincoln's inner motivations add to our understanding of the man and the president? How do their studies advance or hinder historical inquiry? Give examples of how psycho-historians use evidence of motivation legitimately or go too far in their assumptions and conclusions.

SELECTED ANNOTATED BIBLIOGRAPHY

Books

Betts, William W., ed. *Lincoln and the Poets.* Pittsburgh: University of Pittsburgh Press, 1965. A fine survey of poetic contributions to the idealization of Lincoln and creation of the Lincoln myth.

Boritt, Gabor S., ed. *The Historian's Lincoln.* Urbana: University of Illinois Press, 1988. Scholarly evaluations of various parts of Lincoln's life and career by noted historians such as Kenneth Stampp, Richard Current, Dwight Anderson, and Glen Thurow.

Braden, Waldo, ed. *Building the Myth.* Urbana: University of Illinois Press, 1990. A study of the oratory that has memorialized Lincoln. Contributors include Ralph Waldo Emerson, Frederick Douglass, Booker T. Washington, Adlai Stevenson, and Mario Cuomo.

Burlingame, Michael. *The Inner World of Abraham Lincoln.* Urbana: University of Illinois Press, 1994. From the many interesting chapters in this book, you have read selections from two: "Lincoln's Midlife Crisis" and "I Used to Be a Slave." Using hard facts and statements from Lincoln, Burlingame offers informative psychological insight into the man and the president.

Catton, Bruce. *Reflections on the Civil War.* Garden City, N.Y.: Doubleday, 1981. A collection of selections from Catton's many books on the Civil War. Particularly good is a commentary on Lincoln as a strong president (pp. 28 – 33), the kind Catton believes times of crisis call for.

Donald, David H. *Lincoln.* New York: Simon and Schuster, 1995.

Foner, Eric. *Free Soil, Free Labor, Free Men.* New York: Oxford University Press, 1970. A careful and informative study of the ideology of the Republican Party before winning the presidency in 1860, offering a partial explanation of Lincoln's views of freedom and slavery.

Herndon, William H. *Abraham Lincoln: The True Story of a Great Life.* New York: Appleton, 1924.

Lincoln, Abraham. *Abraham Lincoln: Speeches and Writings, 1859–1865.* New York: Library Classics, 1989. Lincoln's major speeches, a collection of his letters, and numerous remarks, both public and private.

———. *Famous Speeches of Abraham Lincoln.* Freeport, N.Y.: Books for Libraries Press, 1969. The most important of Lincoln's public statements, which best express his philosophy and policies.

Oates, Stephen B. *With Malice toward None: The Life of Abraham Lincoln.* New York: Harper and Row, 1977. Perhaps the best one biography of Lincoln, with all the detail, without undue amounts of personal interpretation, needed to form one's own opinion about Lincoln's beliefs and actions.

Sandburg, Carl. *Abraham Lincoln: The Prairie Years* (2 vols.) and *Abraham Lincoln: The War Years* (4 vols.). New York: Harcourt, Brace, and World, 1954. A poetic labor of love, entirely positive, by a man from Illinois who shared Lincoln's humble beginnings and love for mankind.

Articles

Andrews, Peter. "How We Got Lincoln," *American Heritage* (November 1988). The intriguing story of the political maneuvers that made Lincoln the Republican elected president in 1860.

Bellah, Robert. "Religion in America," *Daedalus* (Winter 1967): 1–21. An article that focuses on the American civil religion and Lincoln as its Christ figure.

Carlin Jr., David R. "The Lincoln Myth," *Commonweal* (February 13, 1987): 72–73. An informative analysis of the myth that surrounds Lincoln.

McCollister, John C. "The Faith of Abraham Lincoln," *Saturday Evening Post* (January–February 1983). A light but comprehensive study of Lincoln's own religious beliefs, which influenced his attitude toward his role as president.

McGinnis, Ralph Y. "What Did Abraham Lincoln Stand For?" *Vital Speeches* (May 1, 1979): 439–43. A speech dedicated to the central personal and professional principles that composed Lincoln's philosophy of life and influenced his presidency.

Oates, Stephen B. "Why Should the Spirit of Mortal Be Proud?" *American History Illustrated* (April 1976): 32–41. Using helpful illustrations of life on the frontier, Oates describes the early years when Lincoln practiced law in Illinois.

Wills, Garry. "The Words That Remade America: Lincoln at Gettysburg," *Atlantic* (June 1992). A condensation of Wills's book *Lincoln at Gettysburg* showing how Lincoln's famous speech refocused the Civil War and made postwar America a different place.

CREDITS AND ACKNOWLEDGMENTS

Text

Excerpt from *The Collected Poems of Vachel Lindsay* reprinted with the permission of Simon and Schuster, Inc. Copyright (c) 1925 by Macmillan Publishing Company, renewed 1953.

Excerpt by Dwight G. Anderson from *The Historian's Lincoln: Pseudohistory, Psychohistory, and History*. Copyright (c) 1988 by Board of Trustees of the University of Illinois. Used with permission of the University of Illinois Press.

Excerpt by Stephen B. Oates from *The Historian's Lincoln: Pseudohistory, Psychohistory, and History*. Copyright (c) 1988 by Board of Trustees of the University of Illinois. Used with permission of the University of Illinois Press.

Excerpt by Glen E. Thurow from *The Historian's Lincoln: Pseudohistory, Psychohistory, and History*. Copyright (c) 1988 by the Board of Trustees of the University of Illinois. Used with permission of the University of Illinois Press.

Excerpt by Michael Burlingame from *The Inner World of Abraham Lincoln*. Copyright (c) 1994 by Board of Trustees of the University of Illinois. Used with permission of the University of Illinois Press.

Excerpt from *The Emancipation Proclamation* by John Hope Franklin. Copyright (c) 1963, 1965, 1995 by Doubleday. Reprinted by permission.

Excerpts from pages 252–333 from *With Malice Toward None: The Life of Abraham Lincoln* by Stephen B. Oates. Copyright (c) 1977, 1994, by Stephen B. Oates. Reprinted by permission of Harper-Collins Publishers, Inc.

Excerpts from *Abraham Lincoln: The Prairie Years and the War Years* by
Carl Sandburg, Copyright (c) 1926 by Harcourt Inc. and
renewed 1954 by Carl Sandburg, reprinted by permission of the
publisher.

Photos

xii   Courtesy of The Illinois State Historical Library
8   Courtesy of The Illinois State Historical Library
9   Courtesy of The Illinois State Historical Library
25   Courtesy of The Illinois State Historical Library
68   The Granger Collection, New York
70   Courtesy of The Illinois State Historical Library
95   The Granger Collection, New York
100   Courtesy of The Illinois State Historical Library

INDEX

NOTES

NOTES

NOTES

NOTES

NOTES

NOTES

NOTES

NOTES

NOTES

NOTES

NOTES

NOTES

NOTES